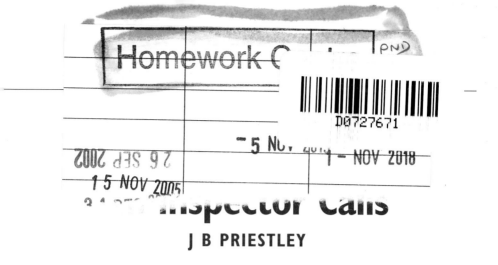

Inspector Calls

J B PRIESTLEY

Guide written by

Stewart Martin

Emily Man IIV

A Literature Guide

First published 1994
Reprinted 1994, 1997, 1998, 1999, 2000 (twice)

Letts Educational
Aldine House
Aldine Place
London W12 8AW
0208 740 2266

Text © John Mahoney and Stewart Martin 1994

This edition edited by Ron Simpson

Self-test questions devised by Sandra Lissenden

Typeset by Jordan Publishing Design

Text design Jonathan Barnard

Cover and text illustrations Hugh Marshall

Design © Letts Educational Ltd

Acknowledgements
The extracts from *An Inspector Calls* by J B Priestley published by Heinemann
Educational Publishers are reprinted by permission of the Peters Fraser and
Dunlop Group Ltd.

British Library Cataloguing in Publication Data
A CIP record for this book is available from the British Library.

ISBN 1 85758 261 6

Printed and bound in Great Britain by
Ashford Colour Press, Gosport, Hampshire

Letts Educational Ltd, a division of Granada Learning Ltd.
Part of the Granada Media Group.

Contents

■ Plot synopsis

The play is set in the fictitious North Midlands industrial city of Brumley in 1912. The wealthy industrialist Arthur Birling and his wife, Sybil, are holding a dinner party to celebrate the engagement of their daughter, Sheila, to Gerald Croft. Gerald is the son of a successful business rival, Sir George Croft, and Arthur Birling is very pleased with the match, partly because of the closer business links which he hopes will follow. Mr Birling talks about his optimism for the future and how he expects Gerald and Sheila to live in a world without class conflict or war.

After the ladies have retired to the next room, Arthur Birling makes a speech about how he believes people should look after themselves and ignore the 'cranks' who say that everybody should take care of everybody else.

A police inspector arrives and says that he is investigating the suicide of a young working-class woman. He shows them a photograph and Mr Birling remembers that she was previously an employee of his whom he sacked for her involvement in a strike for higher pay. Sheila Birling remembers the girl as a shop assistant about whom she made a complaint, because of which the girl was sacked. After this, the Inspector explains, the girl changed her name. Gerald Croft realises that he spent the previous summer with this girl. He confesses this to Sheila and asks her to help him conceal it from the Inspector.

When the Inspector questions Gerald, he admits to the affair, but says that he has broken it off. At this, Sheila hands Gerald back their engagement ring. The Inspector then turns his attention to Mrs Birling and forces her to admit that she knew the girl. The girl, by now pregnant, had approached her charity committee for help only two weeks previously, but Mrs Birling had her turned away. Mrs Birling holds the girl to blame for her own plight, and calls the father of the girl's child a 'drunken young idler', after learning that he had stolen money to support her.

It emerges that Eric Birling is the father of the girl's child and that he stole money from Mr Birling's office to help her. He says that she refused to marry him or to see him again. When Eric learns that his mother turned the girl away, he is furious. The Inspector tells them that they are all partly to blame for the girl's suicide and then leaves. The family then begins to suspect that the Inspector was not genuine. Mr and Mrs Birling are delighted when they telephone the mortuary and discover that there has been no such suicide. As they congratulate themselves on exposing the hoax, and laugh at their children for being taken in, the telephone rings. They learn that a girl has just died on the way to the infirmary – and a police inspector is coming round to question them.

Birling

Arthur Birling

Mr Birling is a successful factory owner, ex-Lord Mayor of Brumley and a local magistrate. He regards himself as reasonable and pays his employees no more and no less than the going rate. He does not punish workers who ask for more money, but simply turns them down on the grounds that it is his duty to keep costs low and prices high.

Mr Birling has little or no imagination, and seems blind both to the consequences of his own actions, and to events in the larger world. He makes predictions about the future – the unsinkability of the Titanic; the impossibility of war; and the promise of technology – which would have been believed by many in 1912, but which would have seemed laughably optimistic to audiences in 1945. Mr Birling can see no reason why nations should go to war and upset the businessmen's quest for profit. It never occurs to him that people might value other things more highly. In many ways, he is a stereotype for his time, and this is true of other characters in the play. Mr Birling is a caricature of the callous heartlessness of a capitalistic businessman.

Birling is proud of his status; he and his wife set great store by his public offices and privileges. So sensitive is Birling about such matters that he even feels a little uneasy about Gerald Croft marrying his daughter, sensing that Gerald's parents may feel that their son is marrying 'beneath himself'. At the end of the play the possibility that he may be deprived of his promised knighthood upsets him far more than anything else.

Mr and Mrs Birling see themselves as upholders of all the 'right' values and as guardians of proper conduct. But both are exposed as self-centred and essentially heartless. They begin by trying to put the Inspector in his place, through emphasising their own position in society. Both try to hide, or hide from uncomfortable truths. As Eric points out, his father is useless in a real crisis. At the end of the play it is Gerald who does all the thinking, not Mr Birling.

It is plain that Birling's motives are not to save Eric from being found out, but to protect himself from social scandal. To do this, he is prepared to distort or ignore the truth. He is blind to this hypocrisy, and indifferent when it is pointed out. Just before the end of the play he happily argues that 'the whole thing's different now', and congratulates himself on having avoided a scandal. Provided their public reputation is safe, people like Mr and Mrs Birling will never change.

Sybil Birling

Mrs Birling is even more hard-faced and arrogant than her husband. She is introduced as his social superior and her manner indicates that she is very conscious of social position, especially her own. She is extremely snobbish, and expects others to show her respect and to defer to her opinions. She resents being contradicted, even when caught out telling outright lies by the Inspector.

Mrs Birling seems genuinely shocked to hear about her son's drink problem, although the information does not surprise Sheila or Gerald. Her concern – shared by her husband – that Sheila should not be exposed to 'unpleasant' things suggests that she regards her daughter as a child. Is Mrs Birling genuinely unaware of what is going on around her, or is she deliberately blind to anything she does not wish to see? Consider how she dismisses the news of Eva Smith's suicide: she cannot see how the death of a 'lower-class' person could be of any interest to the Birlings.

When exposed to criticism, Mrs Birling retreats behind words like 'respectable', 'duty', and 'deserving'. She seems to feel that she is qualified to judge what such words mean. If she feels her own status has been suitably acknowledged, she will be condescendingly generous, but, if not, she will take offence at what she sees as 'impertinence'. She thinks that people from the 'lower classes' have different feelings from her own: they are almost a different species. Eva Smith's pleas for help offend Mrs Birling, because the girl was 'giving herself ridiculous airs' and 'claiming elaborate fine feelings'. Her vindictive attitude towards the father of the girl's child changes dramatically when she learns that he is her own son, clearly illustrating her extreme hypocrisy.

Mrs Birling tries to use her husband's social position to intimidate the Inspector, and is confused when this tactic fails. When the Inspector has left, Mrs Birling forcefully criticises the others for not standing firm against someone who is their social inferior. She argues that if she had been present when the Inspector first arrived, she would have dealt with his impertinence severely.

Try to decide whether, at the end of the play, Mrs Birling has learned to behave in a compassionate or caring way in the future. Perhaps the Inspector's call has only served to harden her attitudes.

Sheila

Sheila Birling

Sheila, the Birlings' daughter, is impressionable, and deeply affected by the Inspector's revelations. She and her brother Eric are the only characters who give any cause for optimism in the play. Sheila has an attractive and essentially honest character, and lacks the cold-blooded attitude of her parents. During the play she sees her father exposed as a hard-hearted employer, her fiancé as a liar who has had a 'kept woman', her brother as the father of an illegitimate unborn child, her mother as callous and unforgiving, and herself as a vain and spiteful girl.

Sheila seems at times almost to be an accomplice of the Inspector, in that she tends to take up his criticism of the other characters, even when he has left the stage. Her parents see this as disloyalty, but Sheila sees no point in concealing either Eric's drink problem or Alderman Meggarty's unpleasant reputation. In this, Sheila is not being vindictive, as Gerald at first mistakenly thinks, but is simply trying, like the Inspector, to get at the truth. Until the arrival of the Inspector, Sheila has been content with socially acceptable indifference to hypocrisy about such things, but Inspector Goole's revelations about her family are a learning experience for her. It is unlikely that she will accept such hypocrisy in the future. Sheila objects to her parents' attempts to protect her from unpleasant truths; '…I'm not a child, don't forget. I've a right to know.' At the end of the play she feels that, whilst for a time it had seemed as though they had learnt something about themselves and their society, once they saw a 'way out', they simply returned to how they were at the beginning.

Because she is more sensitive than the others, Sheila is the first to realise what the Inspector is driving at in his interviews with herself and the others. She sees through the other characters' attempts to cover the truth. She is aware that the Inspector knows all about them and is the first to wonder who the Inspector really is.

Although Sheila identifies with the dead girl, it should be noted that her spiteful complaint against Eva is probably the most indefensible action of all, based merely on her own wounded vanity. The only redeeming feature is that Sheila felt bad about it at the time, regretted it deeply later, and is honest enough to admit her share of the responsibility for Eva's suicide.

Sheila and her brother Eric represent the younger generation which Priestley hopes is still open-minded enough to learn to accept responsibility for others.

Gerald Croft

Gerald's outlook on life is similar to that of Mr Birling. He agrees with the way Birling handled Eva Smith's dismissal: 'You couldn't have done anything else.' Like Mr and Mrs Birling, Gerald's first impulse is to conceal his involvement with Eva; but unlike them, he shows genuine remorse when the news of her death finally sinks in. Moreover, it becomes clear that Gerald helped Eva out of genuine sympathy for her situation and did not take advantage of her in the violent and drunken way in which Eric did. Gerald did make Eva genuinely happy for a time, and in many ways is the least to blame for her death.

At the end of the play, Gerald shows the clearest head in thinking about the identity of the Inspector, is the first to begin devising a way out, and shows initiative in telephoning the infirmary to check if a dead girl has actually been admitted. He also suggests the possibility of there being more than one girl involved.

Does Gerald feel any genuine remorse at the end of the play? He seems to expect Sheila to accept the engagement ring again and asserts that all is now well. The final lines confirm the foolishness of this assumption.

Eric

Eric Birling

During the play, Eric is exposed as a drunkard, the father of an illegitimate unborn child, a liar, a thief and an embezzler.

During the first two Acts, Eric functions mainly as an irritant to Mr Birling's complacency, continually asking what his father regards as silly questions. Mr Birling clearly thinks that his son has not benefited from the expensive education he has given him, perhaps because it was calculated to improve his son's status, rather than develop a critical approach to life.

Eric arouses curiosity with his sudden guffaw in Act 1. This is possibly an indication that he knows something about Gerald, because Sheila has just been scolding Gerald for neglecting her in favour of his work. Curiosity about Eric turns to suspicion later, when he breaks off in mid-comment – he was about to say that he remembered that women find clothes important. We begin to think that Eric has something to conceal.

Eric seems hostile towards his parents, especially his father. This contrasts with his sister, whose criticisms seem more balanced and whose motives are easier to understand. Eric finds his father unapproachable and unloving. This may be why Eva treated Eric, as he himself admits, as if he were a 'kid' and why he responded to her pity. She may have recognised in him a need for affection which she herself shared.

Eric may be a weak and lonely figure, but he is capable of real feeling for others. He is more demonstrative than the others, and at the end he is on the verge of physically attacking his mother in fury at her lack of charity. Remember that, in his eyes, his mother 'murdered' his child and its mother: but remember also that Eric's share of responsibility for Eva's suicide is very great.

Do you think that Eric learned something from the affair? He now sees that 'It's still the same rotten story whether it's been told to a police inspector or to somebody else…. It's what happened to the girl and what we all did to her that matters.'

Inspector Goole

The Inspector is an enigmatic figure. We never even learn his first name. He neither changes nor develops, but frequently repeats: 'I haven't much time.'

Inspector Goole's name is an obvious pun on 'ghoul', a malevolent spirit or ghost. He could be seen as some kind of spirit, sent on behalf of the dead girl to torment the consciences of the characters in the play, or as a sort of cosmic policeman conducting an inquiry as a preliminary to the Day of Judgement, or simply as a forewarning of things to come. Certainly it seems that Priestley did not want to promote a single interpretation of who the Inspector 'really' is. His dramatic power lies in this. To have revealed his identity as a hoaxer or as some kind of 'spirit', would have spoilt the unresolved tension that is so effective at the end of the play.

The stage directions for the Inspector talk of 'an impression of massiveness, solidity and purposefulness' and indicate that 'He speaks carefully, weightily, and has a disconcerting habit of looking hard at the person he addresses before actually speaking'. There is an air of menace about him and, unlike all the other characters, he does not deviate from his moral position. He is single-minded in pursuing his chosen line of investigation. He alone is certain of his facts. These facts are questioned by the other characters only after he has left. Whilst the Inspector is present, nobody challenges his version of events.

The scope and range of Inspector Goole's questions surprises the others. He makes judgements about their characters which they feel are unusual in a police inspector. He undermines their complacent assumption that they are respectable citizens. Each of them finds this a shattering experience.

Those characters who resist telling the Inspector the truth suffer more than those who are more open. The Inspector says to Gerald '…if you're easy with me, I'm easy with you.' Notice that he makes no judgement upon Gerald, and deliberately tries to stop Sheila from blaming herself too much. However, he begins to lose patience with

Mr Birling: 'Don't stammer and yammer at me again, man. I'm losing all patience with you people.' Mrs Birling resists the truth the most, and the Inspector is accordingly harshest with her: 'I think you did something terribly wrong…'.

The Inspector persuades characters to reveal things which they would rather were not known. Sheila points out that there is something about the Inspector which makes them tell him things because they feel that he already knows. The most dramatic example of the Inspector's ability to put his finger on untruth is when he directly accuses Mrs Birling of being an outright liar.

Inspector Goole has several functions in the play. He acts as the story-teller, linking the separate incidents into one coherent life-story. He often supplies dates or fills in background. He also behaves like a father-confessor to each character, encouraging them to acknowledge their guilt for Eva's suicide, and to repent. Significantly, the Inspector himself neither forgives nor punishes. Each character is made to face up to the fact that they must find the courage to judge themselves: only then will they have learned enough to be able to change.

Sometimes the Inspector behaves as the voice of social conscience: 'You see, we have to share something. If there's nothing else, we'll have to share our guilt.' He points out that social responsibilities become greater as privileges increase. He also plays the traditional role of a policeman in a 'whodunnit' story, slowly uncovering the truth through careful questioning, piecing together evidence with shrewd insight. But in a traditional 'whodunnit' mystery the identity of the criminal would be revealed: here, each character is shown as an accomplice to murder, though not one of them has done anything to Eva Smith which a court of law would describe a crime.

Is the Inspector's investigation successful? There is a possibility that Eric and Sheila may have learned enough to change their ways, but the others, even at the end, strongly oppose such changes. Post-war audiences of 1945 would have appreciated the Inspector's prophecy of a lesson that 'will be taught… in fire and blood and anguish'.

Eva Smith

Eva Smith dominates the action invisibly. By the end of the play she is as familiar as the other characters. Eva was very pretty, had large dark eyes and soft, brown hair. She was lively, intelligent, a good worker, warm-hearted, mature and, at twenty-four, about the same age as Sheila.

Eva is depicted as the innocent victim of selfishness. She was a good worker, both at the Birlings' factory and in the shop, but was sacked because of victimisation. She was affectionate towards Gerald, but was abandoned when she became inconvenient. She was a compliant outlet for Eric's sexual needs and loneliness, but was also made an accomplice to theft and pregnant by him. Eva was an outlet for Mrs Birling's 'respectable' feelings of charity, but was discarded as unworthy of help when she did not pander to Mrs Birling's self-importance.

Each incident illustrates that Eva is easy prey for 'respectable' society. In spite of the way society treats her, she shows kindness and sensitivity beyond the reach of the others. Although the victim of exploitation, she refuses to treat others as they have treated her, even though she is in a position to create scandal for them all. As Eva Smith's fortunes sink she is revealed as increasingly noble, the complete opposite to the other characters, except for Sheila and, to some extent, Eric. There is an affinity between Eva and Sheila: Sheila might have suffered the same fate as Eva, had not luck given her a more privileged position in society.

Eva Smith and her fictitious counterpart, 'John Smith', represent ordinary people who can be destroyed by indifference when society fails to grant them the right of basic human dignity.

All of the above assumes that Eva Smith is one person. By assembling all these events and characteristics into one life story, J B Priestley creates sympathy in the audience and in some of the play's characters. We and they can see a hopeful young life destroyed by their complacency, selfishness and thoughtlessness. In terms of the 'real' characters in the play, their actions were *potentially* as damaging even if Eva Smith is a composite created by the Inspector.

◼ J B Priestley (1894–1984)

John Boynton Priestley was one of the most popular, versatile and prolific authors of his day. Though he may not have produced an unquestioned masterpiece, his work in many fields of literature and thought, written from the 1920s to his death, is still highly valued. The best-known of his sixteen novels, *The Good Companions* (1929), which has since been adapted for stage, film and television, tells the story of a company of travelling actors and presents a warm, perhaps sentimental picture of England. His works of popular history and literary criticism are numerous, reaching a climax with the ambitious *Literature and Western Man* (1960).

However, it was as a playwright and as a political and social thinker that J B Priestley was especially important, and certainly these two aspects are what matter most in our study of *An Inspector Calls*. J B Priestley wrote some 40 plays, of which maybe 8 are still performed with some regularity. There are two types of play for which he is especially remembered. One type is regional and nostalgic: plays set in his native Yorkshire at some time before World War One. The most popular of these is undoubtedly the boisterous comedy, *When We Are Married* (1938). The second group of plays are the so-called 'time plays' such as *Dangerous Corner* (1932) and *I Have Been Here Before* (1937), in which themes of fate, responsibility and personal choice are presented by the use of chronological devices. To what degree does *An Inspector Calls* belong to one or both of these groups of plays? See the section **An Inspector Calls: 1912–1945.**

Politically J B Priestley was a patriotic socialist whose love of his country could appear nostalgic, but who was passionately convinced of the need for social change to benefit the poor. During the Second World War his weekly broadcasts were highly influential and expressed his faith in the ordinary people of Britain. In the last year of the war Priestley was writing *An Inspector Calls*, which he saw as a contribution to public understanding which might lead to a Labour election victory after the war (as happened in 1945).

'We have to fight this great battle not only with guns in daylight, but alone in the night, communing with our souls, strengthening our faith that in common men everywhere there is a spring of innocent aspiration and good will that shall not be sealed.' J B Priestley, 1940.

■ *An Inspector Calls*: 1912–1945

It is very easy just to see *An Inspector Calls* as a period piece set in 1912. There are many ways in which it resembles plays set in the North of England in late Victorian times or in the years before World War One: plays like *Hobson's Choice* (written by Harold Brighouse in 1916, set in Salford in 1880) or Priestley's own *When We Are Married* (set in his birth-place of Bradford) deal with domineering businessmen and local politicians whose weaknesses and failings of character are exposed. These are both comedies; *An Inspector Calls* is not, but characters, settings and the use of dramatic revelations are similar. Interestingly enough, many productions of An Inspector Calls set the play in Yorkshire, Priestley's home territory, though 'Brumley, an industrial city in the North Midlands' sounds more like Birmingham than Bradford.

However, *An Inspector Calls* is at least as much about 1945 as about 1912. Despite Mr Birling's smugness about the future, the history of Britain from 1912 onwards was far from trouble-free. The First World War began in 1914, to be followed by a time of severe industrial unrest: in 1926 there was a General Strike, prompted by cuts in miners' wages. At the same time the Labour Party grew in power, without ever establishing a lasting government. There was mass unemployment in the Depression years and the rise of Fascism (notably in Hitler's Germany and Mussolini's Italy) brought international unrest and fear throughout the 1930s. The Government was seen to be doing little about these problems, with Prime Minister Chamberlain's attempts to appease Hitler (avoid war by negotiation and, too often, giving way to his wishes) being particularly ineffective. During the Second World War (which began in 1939) many people became convinced that, after the great struggle against Fascism, we had to try to create a new fairer world in peacetime. J B Priestley's war-time broadcasts expressed this strongly, and so does *An Inspector Calls*. He goes back to a time of great confidence (1912) to show how a fair and just society depends upon compassion and responsibility for our fellow citizens. From 1945 to 1951 the new Labour government attempted to put this into practice.

So *An Inspector Calls* can be seen as a sort of 'time play'. One advantage of this is a fairly straightforward use of 'hindsight'. In particular, when Mr Birling, early in Act 1, gives his account of how things can only get better, he is spectacularly wrong about everything. The *Titanic* will not even complete its maiden voyage, but he is equally far from the mark on general trends. He predicts that: war with Germany will not happen (it started two years later); there will be no problems with labour relations (General Strike in 1926); in 1940 all will be 'peace and prosperity' (Britain was under constant air attack). This is fairly amusing: the audiences at the end of the war must have appreciated the irony of peace and prosperity in 1940. However, it also serves to suggest that Birling is talking nonsense about other things, as when he says a man has to look after himself and take no responsibility for others. In considering *An Inspector Calls* as a 'time play', we should take note of a remarkable production which opened at the Royal National Theatre in 1992, which made a supposedly 'old-fashioned' piece one of the most popular and thought-provoking plays of the 1990s. After international acclaim and countless awards, the production was still running in the West End at the end of 1997. Rather than a realistic 1912-style dining room, the set was of a grand house (finally split apart) set in the middle of war-time destruction, with the 1940s poor surrounding the smug conversations of the Birlings. Inspector Goole came from this 1940s world, giving yet another possible interpretation of him: a sort of 'Spirit of the Future'. The world of the Birlings literally collapsed around them.

This is by no means the only way to stage *An Inspector Calls*, but it served several excellent purposes. It emphasised that the play is not just about 1912, but about 1945 and even later, as when Margaret Thatcher said 'There is no such thing as society' in 1987. It stressed that the world of the Birlings would collapse 'in fire and blood and anguish', as the Inspector says. It focused attention on the moral and political messages, not just the characters and story. It is also worth remembering that, when *An Inspector Calls* was first staged in Moscow in 1945, the staging was not realistic.

Whatever the production, *An Inspector Calls* can (rightly) be seen as many things and still remain a highly effective thriller, a unique form of 'whodunnit'.

■ The structure of *An Inspector Calls*

The drama unfolds in one place (the Birling's dining room). The action is straightforward, without any complicating subplots, and the passing of time on stage is the same as in the theatre: that is, the events depicted in the play actually take up about the same amount of time as passes in the theatre. The breaks between Acts are not allowed to disturb the action of the play and are not used to change the setting. This makes the action of the play realistic and convincing, concentrates the attention of the audience and makes the ending all the more startling.

In Classical Greek drama, it was regarded as essential to observe the **Three Unities**. The Unity of Place is clear enough: the location of the action stayed the same. The Unity of Time was eventually regarded as having a 24-hour time span, but in its purest form meant that (as here) stage time and real time were identical. The Unity of Action meant that there was only one plot; no sub-plots as in Shakespeare. Priestley has produced a textbook example of the Three Unities. The play is even short enough (about an hour and three-quarters) for some productions to play without an interval, thus increasing the sense of unity.

Notice how everything which actually happened to Eva Smith is described or reported to us. All these events – the strike and sackings, the pickup in the Palace bar, the 'love-nest' in Charlie Brunswick's rooms, the rape by Eric, and the interview with Mrs Birling – happen 'off-stage'. In this sense, the Inspector acts like a Chorus in a Greek play. From time to time he sums up what has happened, comments on the characters, and explains to everyone the lessons to be learnt. This includes the audience, who can see their own faults reflected in the play's characters. This was another very old dramatic tradition which was thought to make for a good play. Would it have made the play more or less effective if we had actually met Eva Smith, actually seen the things which happened to her? Would it have lessened the effect of what the Inspector says? Would we still have needed the Inspector at all and, if not, could we be sure that the lessons of the play would have been understood by everyone?

■ Themes in *An Inspector Calls*

Lies

Lies

Lies abound in *An Inspector Calls*. Characters lie to each other, to the Inspector, and to themselves. These lies are not confined to simple misrepresentations of the truth, as when Mrs Birling denies ever having met Eva Smith: some characters begin to see their whole lives as lies. The lies have formed the basis for their relationships with others and with themselves, and they see that they need to begin again, from a standpoint of truth. Other lies in the play concern the way people define things like 'respectability' or 'truth'. This kind of lie is what we normally refer to as 'hypocrisy'.

Love

Love

Several kinds of love are depicted in the play: the husband-and-wife love of the Birlings; the (supposedly) romantic love of Gerald and Sheila; the filial love of parents; the family love of brother and sister; and the Inspector's love of truth. Other attributes of love are shown, such as affection, gratitude, loyalty and sexual feeling. Priestley invites examination of these different expressions of human love and you should try to decide how sincere they are.

Pride

Pride and status

The play also shows how true it is that pride comes before a fall – especially the false pride shown by some of the characters. Pride is revealed as being often rooted in shallow soil, with no substantial base. Only by abandoning false pride can characters arrive at an honest relationship with themselves and each other – but some are unwilling to do this. Their pride has become a self-perpetuating fantasy.

Some characters in the play attach great importance to social status. For them, it is so precious that nothing must threaten it. Social class defines the value of human beings. A high social class insulates these characters from the unpleasantness of reality. Birling panics at the prospect of having his son's or his wife's actions made public. He is clearly terrified by a scandal which would irretrievably damage the Birlings' status. Eva Smith, who is working-class, is seen by some characters as having little value as a human being. The play invites us to question the false reality generated by this attitude.

Responsibility

The play points out the need for a sense of personal responsibility in every member of society: responsibility not only for individual actions, but also for the way actions affect others. The Inspector voices these views most strongly, but is joined by Sheila and, to a lesser degree, Eric. In a sense, these characters act as the communal conscience of the other characters. The opposite view is expressed by Arthur Birling, whose driving concern is self-interest.

Responsibility

Different characters react to their guilt in different ways, when it is revealed to them. Not all show remorse or shame, and some are so hardened that they refuse even to accept that remorse is appropriate. There is a tendency for the younger people to be most likely to show remorse. Priestley suggests that wrongdoing is rather like a disease, eating away from inside. The characters must realise, accept and be responsible for the true results of what they have done, if they are to recover their humanity. Remorse is essential before healing can begin.

Essays/Examiner's tips icon

This icon is used to draw attention to a section of the **Text commentary** that is particularly relevant to either **How to write a coursework essay** or to **How to write an examination essay**. Each time it is used, a note identifies which section it relates to and adds a comment, quotation or piece of advice.

■ Text commentary

Act 1

A dinner party is in progress

Arthur Birling, a prosperous industrialist, holds a celebratory dinner to mark the engagement of his daughter Sheila to Gerald Croft, the son of an even more prosperous business rival of Birling's, Sir George Croft.

Sheila Birling is a little put out because Gerald stayed away from her all the previous summer, although he says it was only because he was busy at the works. Sheila's brother, Eric, suddenly guffaws at this point, and she accuses him of being 'squiffy' (slightly drunk), which he denies.

Arthur Birling toasts Sheila and Gerald. Sir George and Lady Croft are abroad and so cannot be present, but they have sent a cable. Mr Birling says that this night is the happiest of his life, and looks forward to cooperation between his company and Sir George's.

The dining-room of a fairly large suburban house,...

The entire play happens in this room, on one night during the first week of April in 1912. The room is 'substantial and heavily comfortable, but not cosy and homelike'. The Birling household is materially well-off, but only superficially happy and united.

BIRLING: Giving us the port, Edna?...

Mr Birling is at pains to explain that the port is exactly the same as that bought by Gerald's father. Birling sees Sir George Croft as his social superior, and his comment about the port shows he is a social climber. He wishes to enlarge his self-importance, but does so by going through the motions, rather than doing anything really worthwhile. He may no longer be an alderman, or Lord Mayor, but he makes sure that everyone knows that he

Pride

used to be. It is almost the first thing he and his wife point out to new acquaintances, along with the facts that he is a local magistrate and a 'hard-headed', successful, businessman.

Character

An excellent early summing up of the 'characteristics of their class' demanded in the essay on page 58.

SHEILA [*half serious, half playful*]: Yes – except for...

Sheila introduces the first of several incidents which are at odds with the happy atmosphere. These indicate that unpleasantness may lurk beneath the surface of the Birlings' apparently happy family life.

SHEILA: You're squiffy

Sheila accuses her brother Eric of being somewhat drunk. This forewarns us

about his parent's ignorance of his drinking habit. Mrs Birling's reaction shows her marked sense of propriety. Eric's reply and Sheila's comment suggest that there are things about both of them which their parents do not know. Sheila and Eric both use slang expressions which contrast with the language used by their parents. This helps to emphasise their youth and liveliness.

Eric

Each character uses language and speaks in a manner which helps to reveal his or her personality. Compare, for example, the pompous language of Birling with the clipped and incisive style of the Inspector, or the arch and stuffily condescending tone of Mrs Birling with Sheila's blunt and emotional manner. Such things not only affect the way we see each character, but also how we respond to what each says, how much weight we give it, and how far we are convinced by it.

BIRLING: No, we won't. It's one of...

Mr Birling is fairly ignorant of historical and political realities. All he can see

is that he is a successful businessman, alderman, friend to the Chief Constable, ex-Lord Mayor and past greeter of Royalty, who is about to go up in the world.

Mr Birling is happy because Crofts Limited and Birling and Company may one day work together 'for lower costs and higher prices'. Birling seems to regard the marriage of his daughter almost as a commercial arrangement.

Birling

Gerald gives the ring to Sheila

Amidst the toasts, Gerald produces an engagement ring which he gives to Sheila.

Mr Birling makes a speech in which he stresses his 'hard-headed' approach to life, and says that the world (apart from Russia) is in for a time of increasing prosperity. His speech is optimistic. He dismisses the possibility of war and praises the latest advances in technology, such as aeroplanes and the latest wonder in ships, the Titanic, due to sail 'next week'. He says that the future is bright and that the children of Sheila and Gerald will live in a world which will have forgotten class-conflict and war scares. This speech places the action of the drama precisely in time; the Titanic sailed on her maiden voyage from Southampton on Tuesday, 10th April, 1912.

GERALD [*smiling*]: Well, perhaps this will help...

Gerald

Gerald produces an engagement ring. He offers it to Sheila again at the end of the play, although her reaction then is very different to now. Notice how the ring is the one which Gerald wants Sheila to have, not one which she may have chosen. The play abounds with such subtle touches, which fill in character and background. What is being suggested here about the relationship between Gerald and Sheila?

ERIC: Steady the Buffs!

Eric

Sheila, the most emotionally demonstrative character in the play, shows her pleasure at the engagement ring by kissing Gerald. It is interesting that Eric remarks upon Sheila's behaviour here, because he himself has an explosive outburst of emotion at the end of the play. The other characters are more restrained. Eric's comment 'Steady the Buffs!' is a colloquialism. The Buffs (so-called because of the colour of their uniforms) were the East Kent Regiment. The phrase with its military meaning of standing firm against the enemy was first used by Rudyard Kipling. However, it soon became a slang phrase meaning, 'Don't go too far'. Eric is therefore asking for more self-control from Sheila. By the end of the play it is clear that Mr and Mrs Birling, and Gerald, are emotionally stifled by their self-control, whereas Eric nearly loses all his.

MRS BIRLING [*smiling*]: Well, it came just at ...

Mrs Birling's admiration of Gerald's cleverness is echoed by her husband at the end of the play. There are many parallels like this in the play's construction which help bind it together.

BIRLING: Glad you mentioned it, Eric...

Mr Birling explains at length his uncomplicated idea of the world. His vision is sunnily optimistic. He dismisses the prospects of war, strikes and other problems in a self-satisfied way. The world is a comfortable place for Mr Birling.

Morality

Birling is given every chance early on to reveal his selfish anti-community feelings as a 'hard-headed practical businessman' interested only in profit.

The Birling family is introduced as confident, united, assured, prosperous and self-righteous. Later in Act 1, much of this confidence is shown to be completely unjustified. Each of the characters is made to contrast with at least one of the others. Even Mr and Mrs Birling, who are in many ways the most alike in attitude, have obvious differences.

BIRLING: Just let me finish, Eric...

Mr Birling's trust in technology is illustrated by his reference to contemporary inventions and 'progress'. But it is shown that his optimism is no more 'unsinkable' than was the *Titanic*, which he mentions with such pride.

It is easy to laugh at Mr Birling with the benefit of hindsight. History tells us that his trust in the technology of 1912 is as sadly misplaced as is his assertion that there will never be another war. Birling's insistence here on the importance of 'facts' is ironic in the light of later events. He proves to be the most reluctant to face uncomfortable facts later in the play.

But Priestley is not content simply to mock the stupidity of people who think like Birling. He also shows how unthinking and unquestioning Birling's optimism is. It is this refusal of the characters to question, or to understand the consequences of their actions which the Inspector later challenges.

The ladies retire to the next room

When the ladies leave the men to the port and cigars, as was the custom, they take Eric with them, leaving Mr Birling alone with Gerald.

BIRLING: Thanks. [*Confidentially*] By the way, there's something...

Birling explains how he understands Lady Croft's reported feelings concerning Sheila. Notice how this is something which Birling seems to take for granted, assuming that such concern should be 'only natural'. What does this reveal about Birling's views on what is 'natural' in human relationships?

Birling hints at a knighthood

Mr Birling hints that he expects to get a knighthood in the next Honours List, and that this may ease the concern he thinks Mrs Croft feels about the match. Mr Birling jokes that all should be well for his knighthood, so long as his family behaves itself and does not get into the police courts.

Eric joins the other men, having left the ladies talking about clothes. Mr Birling remarks that, to women, things such as clothes are tokens of self-respect. Eric lets slip 'I remember—', but catches himself before he says any more. Mr Birling, in an amused tone, says he expects Eric has been up to something, like many young people who have more money and time than he did when he was young. In another speech, he sets out his basic belief that a man should look after himself and his family, and take no notice of the 'cranks' who say that everybody should care for everybody else. At this moment the front door bell rings.

GERALD [*laughs*]: You seem to be a nice ...

Gerald's joke turns sour as the play proceeds, as attention becomes increasingly concentrated on much which 'seems to be' pleasant and attractive.

ERIC [*eagerly*]: Yes, I remember-.

Eric

Eric starts to say something but suddenly breaks off, becoming confused. Mr Birling and Gerald are faintly amused by this, but the audience's curiosity is aroused – what special knowledge does Eric have of women and their clothes? Why does he suddenly refuse to go on?

Love

Later it becomes clear that Eric's comment relates to his relationship with Eva Smith. Notice how Mr Birling's rather patronising remark about Eric is shown to be ironic in the light of later disclosures. The conversation between Birling and Gerald has been 'man-to-man'. Eric has been described as only a 'boy'. Birling remembers that when he was young, he and his friends were worked hard and kept short of cash, but 'we broke out and had a bit of fun sometimes'. This, together with Gerald's reply, 'I'll bet you did', contains the suggestion that the 'fun' they had was with women.

Given what is later revealed about Gerald's behaviour towards Eva, his innuendo here is quite in character. Birling, on the other hand, adopts a sanctimonious and hypocritical attitude when he learns of his son's relationship with Eva.

BIRLING [*solemnly*]: But this is the point...

Responsibility

Mr Birling expresses his philosophy that 'a man has to mind his own business and look after himself and his own'. The events of the play show this to be unworkable. Immediately, one of those 'cranks', whom Birling has just been sneering at, arrives – as Inspector Goole calls.

The doorbell rings – an Inspector has called

Mr Birling is still a magistrate, and he and Gerald joke that the Inspector's visit may be about a warrant – that is, unless Eric has been up to something! Eric becomes uneasy and Mr Birling begins to suspect something, as Inspector Goole is shown in. Mr Birling does not recognise him, although he knows the local police quite well. The Inspector admits that he has just been transferred, and has come about a young woman in the infirmary who has swallowed disinfectant to kill herself. The Inspector knows a lot about her because she left a letter and a sort of diary which reveal that she used more than one name. Her original name was Eva Smith, and she used to be employed in Mr Birling's factory.

After the Inspector's entrance, nothing will be quite the same again in the Birling household. This is a good point to take stock of what you have learned about the Birling household up to now, because the rest of Act 1 undermines most of what has been presented to us as 'reality'.

ERIC [*Who is uneasy, sharply*]: Here, what...

Eric

Eric does not share the joke between Mr Birling and Gerald. He attracts attention, and then suspicion, by his evident alarm at the news of the Inspector's visit. This clever touch by Priestley alerts us to the possibility that Eric has something to hide.

Character

The group characteristics are not fully shared by Eric: his unease at his secret, his lack of respect, even his speech-patterns mark him down as somewhat different.

BIRLING [*after a pause, with a touch of impatience*]: ...

Birling

Birling is becoming impatient with the Inspector. Notice how Gerald and Birling are not at first worried by his visit. They regard the police as their protectors, but also as their servants. This is why, later on, Mr and Mrs Birling take such sharp exception to the way the Inspector speaks to them.

Birling recognises the girl in the photograph

Mr Birling recollects, after prompting from the Inspector, that the girl left his factory about two years previously, at the end of September 1910. He can see no connection between this and the girl's suicide, but the Inspector seems doubtful about this.

GERALD [*showing annoyance*]: Any particular reason why I...

Inspector Goole

Gerald is irritated that the Inspector refuses to let him see the photograph. The Inspector says that he likes to work this way: 'One person and one line of inquiry at a time'. Gerald is not altogether convinced, and the Inspector's tactic, which he repeats throughout the play, annoys people more than once.

At the end of the play Gerald realises that, by never allowing two people to see the photograph at the same time, the Inspector may have used several different photographs. This is an example of Priestley's dramatic skill.

GERALD: Look here, sir. Wouldn't you rather...

Why does Gerald say this? Is it just good manners on his part? If it is, why is this kind of behaviour 'good' manners? Or is it that Gerald thinks that there may be some scandal? If so, what could be his motive for not wishing to hear about it?

Gerald

BIRLING: Oh well – put like that, there's something...

Mr Birling says that he thinks there is something in what the Inspector says, but contradicts this by going on to say that he 'can't accept any responsibility' for the fate of the girl.

Priestley's main argument in the play is that people must accept responsibility for others, whether they like it or not. As Birling points out, this would make life 'very awkward' for some.

Responsibility

ERIC: By Jove, yes. And as you...

Eric reminds his father of his advice that a man should 'mind his own business and look after himself and his own'. In the light of the Inspector's news about the girl's death, this reminder is embarrassing for Birling. It is the first of many embarrassments which he and others will have to suffer, as they come face to face with the truth.

BIRLING; [*surprised*]: Did you say 'Why?'?

Birling takes exception to the Inspector's tone, but his objections are swept aside as the line of questioning continues.

The characters seem so fascinated by the Inspector's revelations that they

do not notice the unusual way in which he speaks to them. Inspector Goole not only asks questions but also comments on the behaviour and attitudes of everyone, and passes judgement in a way which a real police inspector almost certainly would not do.

Inspector Goole

Here, for example, he goes on to agree with Eric that the girl could not simply have gone off and worked somewhere else, as Birling suggests.

We learn of Birling and the girl

Mr Birling recalls that the girl was one of four or five ringleaders in an unsuccessful strike for more money; she was sacked after the strike failed. The Inspector annoys Birling by asking why he sacked her, and Eric sides with the girl, implying that her dismissal was harsh, although Gerald thinks that Birling was right. Birling says he has to keep costs down, and says he dislikes the Inspector's critical tone. Birling points out that he plays golf regularly with the Inspector's Chief Constable, Colonel Roberts, although this does not seem to cause the Inspector any concern. He asks the Inspector whether the girl got into any kind of trouble after she left his works. The Inspector's reply hints at secrets yet to be revealed.

BIRLING: Well, it's my duty...

Birling

Birling sees himself as a hard-headed, no-nonsense employer. His workers are paid the going rate, no less and no more. He is determined to protect his own interests, and those of others like him. His attitude towards strikers is unsympathetic. Those he sees as trouble-makers are given the sack. He has no regrets about what he did to the girl, and is offended by the Inspector's attitude. Eric expresses faint reservations, but his father rounds on him forcefully and tells him to keep out of it.

Responsibility

Notice Birling's revealing use of the word 'duty'. A duty is normally thought of as something which people do for legal or moral reasons, something which binds them to their obligations. Clearly, Birling has no legal obligation to keep labour costs down; presumably then he sees it as a moral obligation. This tells us about Birling's morality, and, by implication, about how much value he places upon people.

Examiner's tip

For the question on page 61 the examiner will expect you to explain the extent to which characters accept responsibility; Birling's views on responsibility and duty are therefore important.

ERIC: He could. He could have kept her...

Gerald

Eric consistently takes the opposite line to Gerald, and Mr Birling finds this increasingly irritating. Notice how Priestley has made the voice of conscience come, appropriately, from inside the family, not from the outsider, Gerald. Is there anybody else in the play who acts as a kind of 'conscience' for the others?

INSPECTOR: They might. But after all it's better...

Responsibility

The Inspector points out that it is better for people to ask for the earth than to take it. The implication is that some people – like Birling – take everything and leave others with little. Understandably, Birling is offended at being accused of being some kind of thief.

BIRLING: Perhaps I ought to warn you...

Pride

Birling is proud of being 'somebody' in the local community. This is not the first time he has refered to his friendship with Chief Constable Roberts. What does all this tell you about the Birlings? Do you think that all the prominent people they mention would be as ready to draw attention to their friendship with the Birlings?

INSPECTOR: No, I've never wanted to play

The Inspector's deliberate misunderstanding of Eric provides a lighter moment. This provides a contrast to the serious revelations which follow. Do you think the Inspector is making fun of Eric? Or does he think that Eric's expression of sympathy is simply 'good manners' and therefore insincere?

BIRLING [*rather angrily*]: Unless you brighten your ideas...

Birling says it is about time Eric 'learnt to face a few responsibilities'. This

Responsibility

tellingly ironic remark illustrates Birling's hypocrisy. Just a few moments before, Birling denied any responsibility for the girl's fate. Throughout the play, Birling is increasingly desperate to avoid 'facing a few responsibilities'.

The Inspector points out that the girl did not exactly become a prostitute. In what ways was she treated as such by Gerald and Eric?

Sheila returns and learns of the girl's death

Sheila, returning to find out why the men have not come into the drawing-room, discovers the Inspector. Mr Birling becomes annoyed when the Inspector tells her about the suicide. She says the news upsets her, particularly as she has been so happy that night. Birling becomes less cross when the Inspector reveals that all three of them know something about the girl, and that he has called to speak to them all.

The Inspector explains how, after being sacked by Mr Birling, the girl remained unemployed for two months, before she ran out of money, lost her lodgings, and with no one to help her, became desperate. She then had a stroke of luck and got a job at Millwards, a well-known local fashion shop which Sheila goes to. After a couple of enjoyable months the girl was told she would have to leave, as a customer had complained about her.

INSPECTOR [*slowly*]: Are you sure you don't know?

Lies

It is clear that we ought to suspect that Gerald, Eric and Sheila do in fact know something. This device of guilt by implication increases the dramatic tension, and leads us to anticipate more links in the chain of events.

BIRLING [*with marked change of tone*]: Well, of course...

Birling changes his attitude when he is told that the Inspector has come to question everybody. Why is this, do you think? Notice how Gerald has just pointed out that it is what happened to the girl after she left Birling's works which is important.

Birling wishes to settle matters himself, and does not want his daughter involved. Who else behaves in this way, and likes to make decisions for other people?

Birling

SHEILA [*to BIRLING*]: I think it was a mean thing...

Immediately she learns about Eva Smith's dismissal from Mr Birling's factory, Sheila is critical of her father. Throughout the play she consistently acts as the family's 'conscience'. To some extent she is supported in this role by Eric, although he is a much weaker and more evasive character than she is.

Sheila

Why do you think Priestley chose Sheila to fulfil this role? How effective would it have been if the roles of Sheila and Eric had been reversed, with him as the 'conscience' and her as a 'squiffy' ne'er-do-well?

Examiner's tip

'But these girls aren't cheap labour – they're people' Sheila says, as the voice of conscience, of Priestley. Don't let this make you forget her responsibility for Eva's death (see the question on page 61).

There are certain likenesses between Sheila and Eva. This increases our sympathy for Eva by suggesting the happier life she might have had. Sheila perhaps speaks on behalf of the dead girl when she accuses the others of indifference, callousness and so on. The fact that the dead girl made none of these accusations herself while she was alive serves to add more weight to Sheila's attacks.

INSPECTOR [*dryly*]: I've had that notion myself...

The Inspector's pronouncements are not confined to the Birlings. They apply to society as a whole. Priestley achieves this by such statements as: 'it would do us all a bit of good if sometimes we tried to put ourselves in the place of these young women...'. The scope of the play relates to us all. The Inspector's comments are often addressed as much to the audience as to those on stage. This is sometimes true of the other characters.

Responsibility

BIRLING: And then she got herself into trouble...

Notice Birling's choice of words. To what extent is it fair to say that on each occasion Eva Smith met up with one of the play's characters, she got herself 'into trouble'?

Sheila is shown a photograph

Sheila becomes agitated at the mention of Milwards and, when the Inspector shows her a photograph of the girl, she runs from the room in distress. Mr Birling goes after her, intending to tell his wife what is going on.

INSPECTOR [*steadily*]: That's more or less what...

The Inspector makes it clear that his purpose is to establish exactly who it is that has made 'a nasty mess' of Eva Smith's life. Compare this with Birling's attitude. Why exactly is Birling so upset?

Gerald asks to see the photograph. Interestingly, although the Inspector says that he may see it later ('all in good time') Gerald never actually sees it. How different might the rest of the play have been if Gerald had seen the photograph at this point?

Eric would like to go to bed

When Eric says he would like to go to bed, the Inspector advises him against it on the grounds that he may have to get up again soon. Gerald protests that they are respectable citizens, not criminals. The Inspector says that sometimes he cannot tell the difference.

INSPECTOR: Sometimes there isn't as much difference...

The Inspector returns to this key point throughout the play. It is his central 'message'. He wishes to point out to the characters and to the audience, the real nature of responsibility for others.

The Inspector suggests that the line between guilt and innocence is narrower than is commonly assumed. Sometimes it is hard to establish on which side of the line people find themselves.

Character

'We're respectable citizens and not criminals.' Gerald's statement is as much about class as about honesty.

SHEILA [*coming in, closing door*]: You knew it was me...

Sheila is the first to recognise that the Inspector seems to know about them all. Apart from Sheila and Eric, all the characters continue to see Inspector Goole as a police officer or, at the end of the play, as a hoaxer. Sheila is increasingly convinced that he is nothing of the kind, and that his strangeness cannot be explained except in 'other-worldly' terms.

SHEILA [*miserably*]: So I'm really responsible?

Sheila

Sheila is readier than any of the others to admit her guilt and express regret for her actions. The Inspector makes sure that she knows she was only partly to blame.

Contrast Sheila's honest admission of with her mother's confession at the end of Act 2. The confessions of the male characters are similarly different – the younger they are, the easier it is for them to accept the consequences of their actions.

Sheila and the girl in Milwards

Sheila returns and says that she has told her father that she was the customer who complained, that she felt bad about the incident at the time and feels worse about it now. The Inspector says that, like her father, Sheila is only partly responsible for the girl's fate. Sheila explains that the girl, who was attractive, held a dress up against herself in the shop and it was obvious that it suited her. When Sheila tried on the same dress, it didn't suit her and she caught sight of the girl smiling at the other assistant, as if to say that Sheila looked awful. Sheila complained to the manager, saying that the girl had been impertinent. She admits that she was jealous of the girl, but had never done anything like that before.

SHEILA: I'd gone in to try something on...

Eva Smith

Sheila had insisted on trying on a particular dress, even though her mother and the assistant had advised against it. In the event, they had been right; the dress simply did not suit her, and she 'looked silly in the thing'. It is clear that being shown to be in the wrong about the dress put Sheila in a bad mood and she subsequently took this out on the girl.

Compare the different ways in which Eva Smith and Sheila Birling were treated. Eva's activities caused her to be wrongly dismissed by Mr Birling as a 'trouble-maker'. Sheila's actions were clearly much more those of a genuine trouble-maker, but she was immune from punishment because of her social position.

INSPECTOR: And so you used the power you had...

Sheila abused her power in much the same way as her father did when he dismissed the girl from his factory. Between them, Sheila and her father deprived the girl of her livelihood. The next two Acts show how the other characters contributed to the girl's spiritual, moral and physical ruin.

SHEILA: Yes, but it didn't seem to be anything...

Sheila

Sheila is the first to confess her part in the girl's fate. Notice how she immediately expresses regret for what she did and makes only a minimal effort to excuse her behaviour. In this she differs from most of the others. Sheila is also the first, at the end of the play, to protest against the way her parents try to pretend that everything is normal again.

Character

Response to the Inspector is a generational thing: the young are less set in their complacency. Sheila's admission of guilt is obvious in the tone of self-disgust in her narrative.

INSPECTOR [*sternly*]: That's what I asked myself tonight...

Inspector Goole

The Inspector performs the functions of questioner and story-teller in the play. He provides us with the outline of the girl's history, fills in the background where appropriate and sometimes, as here, seems to speak for the audience: 'Well, we'll try to understand why it had to happen. And that's why I'm here, and why I'm not going until I know all that happened.'

We learn of 'Daisy Renton'

The Inspector tells them that, after this, the girl changed her name to Daisy Renton. At this, Gerald becomes agitated and gets himself another drink. As the Inspector leaves the room to find Mr Birling, Gerald admits to Sheila that he knew Daisy Renton, and she realises that this explains his absence the previous summer. Gerald says he has not seen the girl for six months. He wants to keep this from the Inspector, but Sheila says that is impossible, because he 'knows'. The door opens slowly. The Inspector returns, looks at them both searchingly and asks: 'Well?'

INSPECTOR: Where is your father, Miss Birling?

The Inspector now turns his attention to Mr Birling. Priestley cleverly uses

Lies

this device to clear the stage of everyone except Sheila and Gerald, as the Inspector goes with Eric to find Mr Birling. Gerald asks Sheila to keep a secret from the Inspector. She refuses, and when the Inspector returns, his simple, 'Well?', leaves the audience in tense anticipation as the curtain falls on Act 1.

Notice how, with the Inspector out of the room, Sheila takes his role by interrogating Gerald, who comes out of it badly. This is a part which Sheila plays consistently, after her own confession.

SHEILA: Oh don't be stupid. We haven't much time.

Sheila confronts Gerald with his dishonesty just as the Inspector would have done, even echoing the Inspector's urgency: 'we haven't much time'. In spite of Gerald's reluctance to reply, her barrage of questions seems to answer itself. Like the Inspector, she knows.

■ Self-test questions Act 1

Uncover the plot

Delete two of the three alternatives given, to find the correct plot. Beware possible misconceptions and muddles.

The Birling family are having a drinks party/dinner/dance to celebrate Sheila's engagement to Arthur/Eric/Gerald. They pass round the port/chocolates/wine and Gerald gives Sheila a present/ring/necklace. Edna/Gerald/Mrs Birling announces the Inspector, who brings news of the suicide of a young woman 2/3/4 hours previously in the ambulance/operating theatre/Infirmary. She was called Daisy Renton/Eva Smith/Eva Birling and her death was agonising/painless/immediate. Mr Birling recognises her photograph/name/description; he sacked her nearly 2/3/4 years ago because she asked for a wage increase of 2s and 6d/5s/10s. She got a job in a clothes/food/hardware shop, but was dismissed after 2 months/6 months/a year because of a complaint from the manager/another assistant/a customer. It was Sheila/Sybil/Daisy – recognising the photograph, she leaves the room angrily/in confusion/in tears. The Inspector refuses to show Eric/Gerald/Arthur the photograph but Sheila observes that he knows Eva's assumed name, Daisy Renton, and forces him to admit that Eva was his mistress/wife/confidante. She cries/laughs/screams hysterically when he asks her not to reveal this and tells him the Inspector already suspects/has revealed/knows the truth.

Who? What? Why? When? When? Where? How?

1 Who expresses condemnation of Birling's dismissal of Eva?
2 Who makes the longest speeches in the Act?
3 What position of importance has Birling held?
4 What is the connection between Birling and Gerald's father?
5 Why does the Inspector refuse a drink?
6 Why was Eva homeless?
7 When is Eva dismissed from Birling and Co?
8 Where does Eva find work after her dismissal?
9 How does Eva die?
10 How does Sheila react at first to the news of Eva's death?

Who is this?

1 Who is: 'in his fifties, dressed in a plain darkish suit… speaks carefully, weightily, and has a disconcerting habit of looking hard at the person he addresses before actually speaking'?
2 Who is: '…a heavy-looking, rather portentous man in his middle fifties'?
3 Who is: '…not quite at ease, half-shy, half-assertive'?
4 Who is: '…very pleased with life…'?
5 Who is: '…very much the easy well-bred young man-about-town'?
6 Who is: '…a rather cold woman'?

1 'Please, sir, an inspector's called.'

2 '...the way some of these cranks talk and write now, you'd think everybody has to look after everybody else, as if we were all mixed up together like bees in a hive...'

3 'You seem to be a nice well-behaved family...'

4 'She was very pretty and looked as if she could take care of herself. I couldn't be sorry for her.'

Hidden agendas

Every member of the Birling family (and Gerald, about to marry into it) has something to hide, whether or not he or she realises it. Eric is the most aware of his guilty conscience from the beginning of the play, although his secret is the last to be revealed. Can you find FIVE examples in this Act of his restlessness and lack of concentration which reveal this?

Open quotes

It is the Inspector's task to reveal the truth about each character's responsibility for Eva's tragedy, confront deception (particularly self-deception), and peel away layers of self-protection. To do this, he often turns their own words and thoughts against characters. What is his answer to each of the following?

1 SHEILA (*speaking of Milwards*): 'I feel now I can never go there again. Oh – why had this to happen?'

2 BIRLING: 'Why the devil do you want to go upsetting the child like that?'

3 SHEILA: 'if I could help her now, I would –'

4 BIRLING: 'We were having a nice little family celebration tonight. And a nasty mess you've made of it now, haven't you?'

5 GERALD: 'After all, y'know, we're respectable citizens and not criminals.'

Act 2

The Inspector begins to question Gerald

The Inspector looks at Gerald and repeats his question: 'Well?' Gerald sees that he is to be questioned, and tries to get Sheila to leave the room. She refuses.

Gerald says that Sheila simply wants to see him 'put through it' as she was, but she tells him he is mistaken. The Inspector explains that if Sheila does not stay to hear Gerald's story, she will not be able to understand that the girl's death is only partly her fault. He says it is important for people to share their guilt.

GERALD [*with an effort*]: Inspector, I think Miss Birling...

Notice how Gerald echoes Mr Birling's concern to keep Sheila away from anything 'unpleasant'. Is this because he cares for her and does not wish to upset her? Is it because he thinks of himself as her 'older and better', and is being condescending?

Gerald

INSPECTOR: And you think young women ought to...

One characteristic of the Inspector's questioning technique is to turn each character's words and actions back upon him or her. This theme of reversal, of revealing the opposite side, and of worlds turned upside down, runs through the structure of the play.

GERALD: I neither said that nor even...

Gerald protests that he was not implying that Sheila was being selfish or

Sheila

vindictive. Do you believe him? In fact, Sheila accuses herself of these things, probably because she has been made to recognise that these are her failings. Was it her intention to take pleasure in watching Gerald be 'put through it', do you think? Is this why she said that 'it might be better' for her? What other reason could Sheila have for wanting to stay? Remember what the Inspector told her at the end of Act 1 immediately after she said that she was entirely responsible.

INSPECTOR: You see, we...

The Inspector makes another unpolicemanlike comment, which to Sheila

Love

emphasises his strangeness: 'I don't understand about you.' He implies that people should share their innocence and love, but if neither is present, they must share whatever characteristics they do possess. At the end of the play, Sheila and Eric share an attitude which divides them from the others.

Morality

'You see, we have to share something.' The Inspector is the spokesman for Priestley's morality, not for the Brumley Police.

There is something else implied in the Inspector's comment. The society

Responsibility

in which the Birlings live shares out material riches very unequally. This is made plain at several points. Although some people, like the Birlings and Gerald, have been granted the lion's share of material wealth, they are reluctant to accept a similar-sized share of responsibility for those who have been less generously treated. The Inspector points out that, if this is the case, all that remains to be shared is guilt and blame.

The Inspector's message would have seemed appropriate to post-war audiences, concerned about what kind of a world they should be striving for in the future. The central question of the play is whether Eva Smith's fate was mainly a result of the kind of society which existed in 1912, or simply a result of unchanging human nature.

INSPECTOR [*calmly*]: There's no reason why you should.

The Inspector looks calmly at Sheila as she stares wonderingly at him. Some kind of rapport, or understanding, now exists between them. This is an example of how Priestley involves the audience with characters' feelings and thoughts, and encourages the audience to identify more with some characters than with others and take sides in their arguments.

Mrs Birling returns

Mrs Birling enters, her brisk self-confidence quite at odds with the atmosphere. Sheila tries repeatedly to get her mother to drop her inappropriate 'society' manner, and to understand that feeling pleased with herself will only make matters worse when the Inspector questions her. Mrs Birling takes no notice and continues to behave in a condescending way, accusing the Inspector of being impertinent, and reminding him that her husband was Lord Mayor and is still a magistrate.

SHEILA: You see, I feel you're...

Sheila tries to warn her mother that the more she puts on airs and graces, the worse it will be for her eventually. Do you believe Mrs Birling when she says she does not know what her daughter is talking about? The Inspector comments that 'young ones' are more impressionable, implying that Mrs Birling's attitudes are too ingrained to be changed.

INSPECTOR [*coolly*]: We often do on the young...

The Inspector uses the word 'impressionable'. Do you think Mrs Birling understands him? Notice how Priestley makes this clear to the audience in his stage-directions at this point. What is the Inspector implying here, do you think?

Character
If the young are more impressionable, Mrs Birling's certainty that she is always right remains unmoved. What grounds does she have for that certainty?

SHEILA: I don't know. Perhaps it's because...

Lies

Sheila is beginning to see through her mother's facade of respectability. Mrs Birling's inappropriate use of language – 'impertinent', is highlighted when the Inspector draws attention to another inappropriate word – 'offence'. Mrs Birling condemns herself, simply by the words she uses.

MRS BIRLING [*rebuking them*]: I'm talking to the Inspector...

Pride

Mrs Birling ignores Sheila's warnings and persists in trying to use her social position to intimidate the Inspector. She has already attempted to discredit Eva as one of the 'girls of that class', and has criticised the Inspector as 'impertinent'. She likes to see everyone else as children and herself as parent.

Mrs Birling makes two quite untrue statements about Eric – that he isn't used to drinking and that he is only a boy. It is the signal for the shattering of her illusions.

Eric is exposed as a drunkard

The Inspector asks about Mr Birling and is told that he is looking after Eric. Mrs Birling says Eric has had a little too much to drink because of the celebrations, and becomes upset when Sheila points out that Eric has been drinking too much for the previous two years. Gerald says he has gathered that Eric drinks 'pretty hard'. Mr Birling comes back without Eric, and the Inspector says he will see him later.

MRS BIRLING: But it's you – and not the Inspector...

Mrs Birling is put out because Sheila, not the Inspector, reveals all the embarrassing truths. Although we sense that the Inspector knows a lot more than he pretends, his usual method is to put characters in a position where they have no choice but to admit the truth about themselves.

SHEILA [*rather wildly, with laugh*]: No, he's giving us...

The Inspector is beginning to take over: notice how he crosses Mr Birling's instructions that Eric should go to bed. Both Sheila and Eric now begin to pay more attention to the Inspector than to their own parents. Why do they behave in this way?

We learn of Gerald and the girl

The Inspector questions Gerald, who confesses that he knew Daisy Renton. He met her in a bar at the Palace Variety Theatre in Brumley, where prostitutes were known to congregate, and rescued her from the attentions of Alderman Joe Meggarty, whom he describes as a notorious womaniser and drunkard, to the astonishment of Mrs Birling (though not of Sheila and the Inspector). Gerald and the girl went to the County Hotel for a drink and a chat. The girl told Gerald something about herself but Gerald was unable to get a complete picture about her past life. She was broke and hungry and Gerald made the hotel find her some food.

Gerald and the girl met again two nights later. A friend of Gerald's had gone off to Canada for six months and left Gerald the use of his rooms in the town. Gerald insisted that the girl use the rooms, and gave her money. He makes it clear that he did this without asking for anything in return, but admits that eventually they became lovers, although Gerald did not feel as strongly about her as she did about him. The suggestion is that neither really loved the other; she was grateful, while he was flattered. Sheila is sharply critical of Gerald, but acknowledges his honesty. Gerald explains that the affair ended at the start of September, when he went away on business for a few weeks and the girl left the rooms, with a parting gift of money.

The Inspector says the girl's diary reveals that she went to a seaside place for about two months and, feeling that she would never be as happy again, just wanted to be quiet and remember it. The Inspector allows Gerald, who says he is more upset than he may appear, to go for a walk.

GERALD: I didn't propose to stay long...

What was Gerald doing in a bar which, as he admits himself, is a known haunt of prostitutes and their clients? Is this another example of Gerald's hypocrisy?

Gerald describes his behaviour in snatching the girl away from Joe Meggarty as though he was conducting a rescue mission. Given the way he subsequently used and then discarded her when she became inconvenient, how different do you think Gerald and Joe Meggarty really are?

Gerald

MRS BIRLING [*staggered*]: Well, really! Alderman Meggarty!...

Although Mrs Birling appears shocked to learn of the commonly accepted truth about Joe Meggarty, is it credible that she can have been so ignorant of his reputation if at least three of the six people present thought it common knowledge?

As the play progresses, the most 'respectable' members of the local community are thoroughly discredited. These include: a local Alderman, ex-Lord Mayor and successful businessman; the son of an ex-Lord Mayor; another Alderman; the son of local gentry; and the Chair of the Brumley Women's Charity Organisation. What does this imply about the basic values of a society in which such people rise to positions of importance?

Lies

Morality
Priestley is writing about 1912, but for 1945. He wishes the country were governed differently. Discrediting the old ruling class is consistent with this view.

People like the Birlings have pretensions to 'superiority', which is not just a matter of wealth, but also embraces moral and social values. Mrs Birling's attitude towards the Eva Smiths of this world ('girls of that class') shows that she thinks herself a better human being than they, not merely wealthier.

Pride

One of the mainstays of the Birlings' snobbery is that they mix exclusively with people like themselves. This is why Mrs Birling is so shocked by the revelations about Alderman Meggarty. Later we learn that Gerald Croft and Eric are not so dissimilar to Meggarty in their attitudes towards women (at least on the surface).

The play is set in an age when very high standards were expected from public figures. Even today we expect public figures to live by higher standards than ordinary people. Do you think this is hypocritical? Think about your feelings towards the characters. Are you glad when it looks as though Gerald and Mr and Mrs Birling are going to get their comeuppance? Do you find the behaviour of Joe Meggarty any more offensive than Eric's, or Gerald's?

GERALD: Yes. I asked her questions about herself...

Gerald tells his story at considerable length. The few interruptions are dramatically necessary, to avoid his speech becoming simply a very long monologue. The girl's account of the factory and the shop were, Gerald says, 'deliberately vague'. This vagueness helps the characters to persuade themselves later that several different girls were involved, although this question remains open.

Eva Smith

GERALD [*steadily*]: I discovered, not that night but...

Gerald does not say whether the girl agreed to meet him, or whether she was a willing sexual partner. He says she felt 'grateful', but says it was only natural, under the circumstances. To what extent do you feel Eva Smith was responsible for her own tragedy? After all, she did not have to go on strike, any more than she had to accept Gerald's offer of rooms, or go to the Palace bar, or let Eric take her home. Is this a fair attitude to adopt towards Eva?

Eva Smith

BIRLING [*rather taken aback*]: Well, I only did...

Mr Birling says he dislikes his daughter, 'a young unmarried girl', being dragged into the affair. Birling's hypocrisy is staggering. His description of his

Birling

own daughter perfectly describes Eva Smith, but he adopts entirely different standards when considering Sheila. A little earlier, Gerald did not want Sheila to hear him being interrogated. Gerald may have wanted to save himself embarrassment, but he also clearly wanted to protect Sheila from unpleasantness.

Both Birling and Gerald have completely different standards for women of different classes. In Act 1, they joke about the 'fun' that young men get up to. Their amusement comes from a 'boys-will-be-boys' attitude to sexual relationships. Gerald uses the girl, then discards her, just as Birling did. Eric uses the girl for sex and treats her, as the Inspector says in Act 3, 'as if she was an animal, a thing, not a person'. What does this tell you about the society in which Priestley sets his play?

SHEILA: Yes, and it was I who had...

Lies

Sheila refuses to be treated like a child any longer. She rebels against her father's attempt to cut her out of the conversation. Her sharp, inquisitive tone forces Gerald to admit the truth to himself. The process is shown as painful but necessary: as Sheila says, 'I've a right to know.' The suggestion is that each of us has a similar right to know the truth about ourselves. Gerald owes it to himself to tell the truth.

Morality

Acceptance of responsibility is part of Priestley's moral lesson. Birling and Sheila have forfeited their right to protest or protection by their actions – but only Sheila knows that.

Sheila returns the ring to Gerald; he goes for a walk

Sheila says that although she now respects Gerald more than she did, they will have to start getting to know each other again, because they have become different people. Gerald goes out.

GERALD: I see. Well, I was expecting this.

Gerald

Why was Gerald expecting Sheila to give him his ring back? It cannot be because of what he has done, because he knew all about that before he gave it to her. Look carefully at what Gerald says. Do you think he feels ashamed of what he has done? Do you think he felt ashamed whilst the Inspector was questioning him?

SHEILA: I don't dislike you as I did...

Sheila

Sheila is scrupulously fair. Notice how she gives Gerald credit for his honesty, and accepts that he acted from honourable motives when he first became involved with the girl. She even accepts partial blame for reducing Eva to the state she was in when she met Gerald. She does not say that she is dropping Gerald for good, merely that they are not the same people who sat down to dinner earlier and that they will have to 'start all over again'.

GERALD: I don't think so. Excuse me.

Do you think the Inspector makes much of an impression on Gerald? He does not appear again until the second half of Act 3. During his absence, certain things about the Birlings are revealed, which they are keen to keep hidden when he returns. This technique of making revelations in a character's absence is used several times to develop the story.

The structure of *An Inspector Calls* is very well crafted to maintain the audience's attention and anticipation. There is much use of contrasting moods: the comfortable self-satisfaction of the characters at the opening turns to anxiety, then terror. They sink partially back into complacency as they are offered an escape route – everything has been a hoax – before their security is suddenly undermined again in the final few seconds.

Mrs Birling is shown a photograph

The Inspector shows a photograph of the girl to Mrs Birling, who claims not to recognise her. The Inspector accuses her of lying, and Birling angrily demands an apology. Sheila realises that her mother recognises the girl, and tells her parents they only make things worse by pretending. The front door slams and Birling goes to investigate.

The Inspector questions Mrs Birling about her part in the Brumley Women's Charity Organisation. She admits that she was chairwoman of the committee, which sat two weeks previously. Mr Birling returns to say that the noise of the door must have been Eric going out. The Inspector says he will have to be brought back if he does not return soon, because he is going to be needed.

INSPECTOR [*massively*]: Public men, Mr Birling, have responsibilities

Responsibility

Mr Birling's response to this self-evident truth is astounding: 'possibly', he says. This prefaces a long speech by Sheila, spelling out what has happened so far. In this respect she is acting, as the Inspector sometimes does, like the Chorus in a Greek tragedy. Do you find these passages realistic? Look closely at Sheila's speech. Note the conversational tone and language.

INSPECTOR: Yes, a very good reason. You'll remember...

The Inspector forces Mrs Birling to admit to her part in the girl's suicide, but only after she has lied about knowing her. The Inspector uses the name 'Eva Smith' and Mrs Birling agrees that she had seen her, but that the girl called herself 'Mrs Birling'.

Mrs Birling

We learn of Mrs Birling and the girl

The Inspector resumes his questioning of Mrs Birling by saying that she saw Eva Smith at the committee meeting two weeks previously, where the girl appealed for help. Mrs Birling admits this, and further admits that because the girl called herself Mrs Birling, she was prejudiced against her case. Mr Birling supports her in this. Mrs Birling says that the girl had only herself to blame for her fate, and that she lied about her circumstances: being married, deserted by her husband, and so on. Mrs Birling says that her conscience is clear because the girl was not a deserving case, and that she used her influence to have her application for help refused.

MRS BIRLING [stung]: Yes, it was...

Mrs Birling had felt that the girl had not been respectful enough towards her. Notice how Mrs Birling prides herself on being a good judge of character. She says that it did not take her long to get 'the truth – or some of the truth' out of her. But Mrs Birling resents the way the Inspector probes for

Lies   the truth – or some of it – from the others.

Mrs Birling is confident that she can resist the Inspector's questioning. She is convinced that she has done nothing wrong. Does the Inspector manage to dislodge her from this view? Given Mrs Birling's determined opposition, how does he manage to get her to talk about her part in the affair?

The Inspector says that Mrs Birling is mistaken to think she has done nothing wrong, and reveals that the girl was pregnant. This was why she went to Mrs Birling's committee for help. It is made clear that the father of the child is not Gerald Croft. Mrs Birling knew the girl was pregnant when she turned her down. Sheila, horrified, calls her mother cruel and vile and Mr Birling says it will go against them at the inquest. Mrs Birling points out that she was not the one who sacked the girl from the factory, and that the girl knew who the father was but was claiming 'elaborate fine feelings' and giving herself 'airs'. She also admits that the girl said she did not want to take any more money from the father, because she suspected that he was stealing it.

BIRLING: Look here, this wasn't Gerald Croft –

Notice how this suspicion is raised and squashed at once. Priestley wants the audience to question the motives of the characters and skilfully prevents us travelling up a blind alley. What dramatic advantage is there in ruling out Gerald Croft as the father of Eva's child?

SHEILA [*with feeling*]: Mother, I think it was cruel...

Notice how different the respective reactions of Sheila and her father are here. Sheila denounces the act for what it was, whilst Birling thinks only of the possible scandal if the Press should take up the story.

MRS BIRLING: Whatever it was, I know...

Mrs Birling uses the same expression which the Inspector will use in a moment – she lost 'all patience' with the girl. Ironically, it was the girl who showed tact and delicacy in protecting Eric: Mrs Birling displayed only intolerance and snobbery.

It is impossible to feel any sympathy for the older Birlings, but we are encouraged to feel some sympathy for Eric and Sheila. This simple contrast between generations is made more complex by the inclusion of Gerald.

Gerald

Gerald is a more complicated character than most of the others. His function at different times is to side with the Birlings, to act as a contrast to both 'sides' of the family in some way or other, to represent the 'real' upper class, as opposed to the social-climbers, to fill in narrative background about the girl, and to supply plausible-sounding explanations at the end of the play.

Mrs Birling blames the baby's father

Mrs Birling says that because the girl lied about being married, she may well have lied about other things – so Mrs Birling feels justified in refusing her help. She places equal blame upon the father of the girl's baby, saying that this 'drunken young idler' should be made an example of, because the girl's death is due to him. Even if the story about him stealing money is true, it is still his responsibility, she says, because if he had not stolen the money, the girl would neither have come to the committee nor have been refused help.

MRS BIRLING: Then he'd be entirely responsible –

Mrs Birling is as blind to the irony of what she is saying as she has been to everything else: her son's drinking, the behaviour of so-called respectable figures of the community, and the revelations about the 'real' family life which surrounds her. Just as her rejection of the pregnant girl was a death-sentence for her grandchild, so here her condemnation of the father is a final judgement upon her own son.

Lies

MRS BIRLING [*triumphantly*]: I'm glad to hear it.

Mrs Birling feels triumphant that she has finally cleared herself and outwitted the Inspector. Just as at the end of the play, Priestley here allows a false sense of security to develop, before smashing it to pieces. This is a classic technique of the 'suspense' writer.

MRS BIRLING: Waiting for what?

Mrs Birling asks the Inspector the fatal question. Sheila and the audience know the answer by now. Notice Priestley's skill in using the simple device of the Inspector holding up his hand to focus all the tension on the silence, as Eric enters and the curtain falls on Act 2.

Eric is exposed as the father

Sheila realises that the father of the girl's baby is Eric, and tries to warn her mother, but Mrs Birling presses on, demanding that the Inspector make a public example of the father. When Mr and Mrs Birling finally realise what the Inspector has been leading up to, Mr Birling asks whether the Inspector is saying that his son is the father. The Inspector does not give a direct answer. The front door is heard to open, and Eric enters, looking pale and distressed. He looks around at the others.

MRS BIRLING [*agitated*] I don't believe it. I won't...

Mrs Birling finally realises the truth. Notice how she decides whether or not she will believe something, not on the basis of its truth, but on whether she finds it attractive or plausible.

Does Mrs Birling have any redeeming features? The end of Act 2 reveals her as a fatally flawed woman, unable to cope with the real world. Do you pity her for her blindness, or do you blame her for using her social position to inflict damage on the lives of others?

Mrs Birling

43

Uncover the plot

Delete two of the three alternatives given, to find the correct plot. Beware possible misconceptions and muddles.

The Inspector dismisses Edna/Mrs Birling/Sheila but she refuses to go; she and Gerald bicker/make love/shout at each other. The secret of Eric's drinking/ womanising/smoking is revealed and Mrs Birling is defiant/staggered/heartbroken. Gerald tells how he met Eva in a cinema/a palace/The Palace music hall; she wanted to flirt/talk/tell him her past and he found some food/drink/money for her. He says that he loved her/was attracted to her/felt sorry for her; the affair ended in September/October/November. Gerald leaves to take a walk, saying he will go home/return/try and forget. Mrs Birling pretends not to recognise the girl in the photograph, although Eric/Birling/Sheila realises she is lying. They are interrupted by news of Eric's departure – the Inspector is angry/uninterested/unsurprised and Mr and Mrs Birling angry/defiant/frightened. The questioning continues; Eva was ill/pregnant/had had a child when Mrs Birling was responsible for help being refused/offered/given to her. Mrs Birling describes her story as 'unlikely'/'pitiful'/ 'ridiculous' and thinks that the father of the child should be dealt with 'severely'/'properly'/'leniently'. It is Birling/Sheila/Gerald who first realises Eric is the father; as the curtain falls, he enters, looking 'pale and distressed' and his mother/sister/father gives a little cry.

Who? What? Why? When? When? Where? How?

1 Who was bothering Eva/Daisy in The Palace bar?
2 Who is 'entirely responsible' for Eva's death, according to Mrs Birling?
3 What was Eva's reason for approaching the committee of the Brumley Women's Charity Organisation?
4 What does Sheila give to Gerald before he leaves?
5 Why does Mrs Birling pretend not to recognise Eva's photograph?
6 When did Mrs Birling see Eva?
7 Where did Eva go after the affair with Gerald?
8 How does the Inspector claim to know so much about Eva's life?

Who says to whom?

1 'I never take offence'
2 'I think she had only herself to blame.'
3 'Why are you saying that to him? You ought to be saying it to me'
4 'I feel you're beginning all wrong'
5 'I – well, I've suddenly realised – taken it in properly – that she's dead –...'

Mutual recrimination

Throughout the play, moral judgements are made by the audience on the characters' actions and by the characters on themselves. Who is condemning whom in the following quotations?

(Note that the Inspector is 'impartial', interested only in finding out the truth, no matter which civilised veneers he must pull down in the process)

1 'I think it was cruel and vile' (Act 2)
2 'My God, it's a bit thick, when you come to think of it –' (Act 1)
3 'I think it was a mean thing to do. Perhaps that spoilt everything for her' (Act 1)
4 'I don't think we want any further details of this disgusting affair –' (Act 2)
5 'You're the one I blame for this' (Act 3)

Act 3

Eric enters

Eric knows that everybody else is now aware of his part in things. He is cross that Sheila has told the others about his drinking, but she tells him that he is being unfair – she could have told everyone months before, and has only spoken up now because it is obvious that everything is coming out into the open. Mrs Birling is distressed and Mr Birling feels Sheila has been disloyal. The Inspector wants to hear Eric's side of things.

MRS BIRLING [*distressed*]: Eric, I can't believe it

Why does Priestley save Eric until last? At first the Inspector dealt with each character's involvement with Eva Smith in strict chronological order: Birling, then Sheila, then Gerald. The sudden switch of order is deliberate: how would the climax of the play have been changed if the Inspector had dealt earlier with Eric? If you had been the writer of the play, which arrangement do you consider would have produced the best climax?

SHEILA: No, that's not fair, Eric...

Sheila is now honest enough to have no hesitation in admitting to Eric that she was the one who told their mother about his drinking. But she is also fair-minded enough to see that honesty cuts both ways, and she refuses to let Eric escape without his acknowledging that she had protected him for a considerable time.

Lies

We learn of Eric and the girl

Eric says he met the girl in the Palace bar one night the previous November, when he was drunk. He went home with her, threatening to make a row unless she let him into her lodging, and made love to her, although he remembered nothing about it afterwards. On Mr Birling's instructions, Sheila and her mother leave the room at this point. Eric goes on to tell how he and the girl met several times after this, they made love again, and the girl became pregnant. Although they were both very worried about the pregnancy, Eva refused to marry Eric, because he did not love her. Eric gave her money to live on – about fifty pounds in all.

INSPECTOR: And you made love again?

Love

The Inspector's question produces an interesting answer. The girl was 'a good sport' and Eric 'liked her', although he didn't love her 'or anything'. Compare Eric's relationship with the girl to Gerald's. Compare the words used to describe the way the relationships developed from casual acquaintance into something much more intimate.

ERIC: Well, I'm old enough to be married...

Eric complains that he is being criticised as though he were a child. Mr Birling's reaction to the news of his son's sexual indiscretions is very different from his reaction to Gerald's. Their parents treat Eric and Sheila as though they were still young children. Eric and Sheila have had expensive educations and the best of everything. What have they lacked? How has this contributed to the way they treated Eva?

Character

Eric is again the outsider. Note the gap between the generations and the sense that the respectable middle-classes are above criticism: as many 'fat old tarts' as they want and nothing said!

INSPECTOR: Did she suggest that you ought to...?

Eric's answer to the Inspector's question again shows that the girl had the 'fine feelings and scruples' which Mrs Birling denied her in Act 2. In fact, she had

Eva Smith

a stronger sense of moral responsibility than those who ruined her life and drove her to suicide. She would not marry Eric because she knew that he did not love her. She would not take his money because she suspected that he was stealing it. She did not expose him to his mother, because that would have been blackmail.

Eric is exposed as a thief

Mr Birling demands to know where Eric got the money, and it becomes clear that he stole it from his father's office.

46

BIRLING [angrily]: What do you mean – not really?

Lies

Mr Birling suddenly shows a great interest in the precise use of words and in establishing exactly what has gone on. He is outraged by his son's evasion of the accusation of theft. Eric claims that, because he meant to put the money back, it was not really theft. He is unable to say how he might have returned the money, but Birling sees correctly that this is immaterial anyway.

Sheila and her mother return

Mr Birling tells his wife and daughter that Eric has admitted that he got the girl pregnant, and that he gave her money he had stolen from the office.

The Inspector gets Eric to confirm that when the girl realised that the money was stolen, she refused more. She also refused to see him again, and Eric demands to know how the Inspector knew this. Sheila says that the girl told their mother. Eric, near breaking-point, accuses his mother of being the murderer of her own grandchild.

ERIC: Because you're not the kind of father...

The Birlings are not only callous towards those they perceive to be their social inferiors: they are also inadequate as parents. Birling argues that his son has been spoilt. What precisely does he mean by 'spoilt'? Is this what is wrong with Eric?

MRS BIRLING [very distressed now]: No – Eric – please –

Lies

Mrs Birling's cries of anguish carry little weight with Eric. Her excuse fails to convince, because we have seen already how she stubbornly refuses to see anything which does not fit in with her narrow view of the world. We can see that Eric is correct in his analysis, and that Mrs Birling is expert at ignoring unpleasant facts, even when they are thrust under her nose.

INSPECTOR [taking charge masterfully]: Stop!...

Inspector Goole

The Inspector begins his summing-up. In the 'trial' of the various characters, he has acted sometimes as the counsel for the defence, at other times as the counsel for the prosecution, and now he delivers the verdict of the jury. Who plays the part of the judge?

BIRLING [unhappily]: Look, Inspector – I'd give thousands –

Birling would not pay Eva Smith, a good worker who was about to be promoted to leading operator status, another two shillings and sixpence a week. Now he offers thousands of pounds to put right his mistake. Not only is he offering the money at the wrong time (as the Inspector points out) but also, from a purely financial point of view, he is doing poor business. The sad fact is that Eva deserved the extra money anyway – something which

Responsibility   Birling has never denied.

The Inspector makes a speech – then leaves

The Inspector sums up by saying that there are millions and millions of Eva Smiths and John Smiths 'all intertwined with our lives' and that because people do not live alone, they are 'responsible for each other'. He threatens that if people cannot learn this lesson then they will soon be taught it 'in fire and blood and anguish'. Then he leaves.

Mr and Mrs Birling round on Eric, blaming him for everything, and saying they are ashamed of him. He says he is ashamed of them, too. Sheila becomes angry at the way her parents seem to be ignoring the lesson they should have learnt.

INSPECTOR: But just remember this. One Eva Smith...

Inspector Goole's message is that a great wrong has been committed. Although only Eric has committed a crime in the legal sense of the word, the Inspector has forced them all to see that it is not enough simply to behave in a 'proper' way, according to a 'code of manners'. Notice the biblical tone of

Responsibility   the Inspector's words. What effect is Priestley trying to achieve?

Examiner's tip/Character/Morality

It is hard to imagine an essay that does not make use of the Inspector's great 'fire and blood and anguish' speech. It is central to the themes of guilt and responsibility and to Priestley's moral position.

BIRLING [*angrily to Eric*]: You're the one I blame for this.

The traditional detective story is a recognised type of literature. A type of literature is sometimes called a genre (meaning a kind or a category). But although *An Inspector Calls* begins like a typical detective story or 'whodunnit', it soon becomes clear that this is a very strange 'whodunnit' indeed – because everybody 'dunnit'. Like many of its characters and events, the play itself turns out to be very different from what it had seemed at first to be.

Priestley uses several traditions of a 'whodunnit'. There is an investigation into a murder, a limited number of suspects, some false trails, and a murderer is finally unmasked by a brilliant detective. The audience's enjoyment comes from trying to guess who the guilty party is before the Inspector reveals the answer. But in Priestley's drama, the circle of guilt widens and each character is drawn into the role of villain, rather than eliminated from suspicion.

In *An Inspector Calls*, actions which characters have not previously seen as wrong are revealed as highly immoral by the Inspector. Birling has treated people as cheap labour; Sheila made others suffer because of her childish tantrums; Eric has been a thief and a promiscuous liar; Gerald has lied to his fiancée; and Mrs Birling, Chair of the local charity organisation, has failed to show any charity at all. Each character sees his or her self-justification torn to shreds by the Inspector's questioning.

BIRLING [*angrily*]: Yes, and you don't realise yet...

Lies

Birling's accusation is levelled at Eric and is ironic: of all the characters who fail to realise what they have really done, Mr and Mrs Birling are the two clearest examples.

The Inspector's departure is the signal for recriminations to break out. Significantly, Mr Birling begins this, blaming Eric for everything.

BIRLING [*angrily*]: Drop that. There's every excuse...

Birling is quite correct: every excuse has been made to justify the actions of Mr and Mrs Birling. Why does Birling not now simply own up? Why do he and his wife hold on to their blinkered view of things?

SHEILA: I don't know where to begin.

Sheila

Sheila is staggered at her father's 'it turned out unfortunately, that's all – '. Birling's easy dismissal of the night's events leaves her speechless. But where should Sheila begin? Where should any of us begin, in trying to decide what to do about a world in which this kind of thing can happen?

Character
An effective summary of the impact (or lack of it) of the Inspector on the characters: 'I behaved badly'/'Nothing much has happened'/'You don't seem to have learnt anything'.

ERIC [*cutting in*]: Yes, and do you remember...

Pride

For the second time, Eric reminds his father about his pompous and selfish speech near the start of the play. This makes a dramatic link between the beginning and the end of the play. It is the completion of Priestley's 'circle', within which the action of the play moves. This speech of Eric's is also used to allow Sheila to begin wondering aloud about the real identity of the Inspector.

Was he really an Inspector?

Sheila comments that the Inspector arrived just after Mr Birling told Gerald and Eric that a man should look after himself, mind his own business, and ignore 'cranks' who tell everybody to look after everybody else. Sheila wonders if he really was a police inspector. Mr Birling says that if he was not, this would change everything. Sheila disagrees and Eric sides with her. Birling accuses Eric and Sheila of letting the Inspector bluff them into telling him things he did not really know.

SHEILA: It doesn't much matter now, of course...

Sheila

Alert as ever, it is Sheila who first voices the doubt which will dominate the rest of the action: was Goole a police inspector? Notice how, unlike everybody else except Eric, she takes the position that the question is of no importance now. To Gerald and Mr and Mrs Birling the answer to this question is all that matters.

BIRLING: Then look at the way he talked...

Pride

Birling thinks that it was outrageous of the Inspector to talk to a man of his standing in the way he did. Again he lists his public offices. Birling takes it for granted that these honours confer upon him some kind of special status which means that people must talk to him in a respectful and deferential way.

SHEILA: It's all right talking like that now...

Sheila's comment is both accurate and interesting. But exactly how did the Inspector make each of them confess?

Gerald returns

Gerald returns from his walk. While he was out, he ran into a police sergeant who is an acquaintance of Gerald's. He reveals that their caller was not a real police officer.

BIRLING: The fact is, you allowed yourselves to...

Birling

Birling is the one who is bluffing. Look at the way he immediately panics when the doorbell rings. Mrs Birling turns to her husband for leadership. She tells Eric and Sheila to 'be quiet'. They must let their father decide what to do. Look carefully at how Mr Birling reacts to this. How misplaced is his wife's confidence in him?

MRS BIRLING: The rude way he spoke…

Mrs Birling is more concerned about the way the Inspector addressed herself and her husband than with the truth of what he revealed. She describes the Inspector's manner as 'extraordinary'. As far as she is concerned, there has been nothing 'extraordinary' about her own behaviour, or that of her husband, towards Eva Smith.

> ### Examiner's tip
> For the essay on page 61, you might consider whether the fact that he wasn't a police officer makes any difference; some characters certainly think so.

GERALD [*slowly*]: That man wasn't a police officer.

Birling feels that this news 'makes all the difference'. Gerald agrees: 'Of

Lies

course!' Sheila's acid comment cuts them both: 'I suppose we're all nice people now.'

Dramatically, Gerald's revelation is crucial, because it allows some of the characters to believe they are off the hook. In a sense, this is the acid-test of what each has learned. Study closely what each of them does next.

There is no 'Inspector Goole'

Birling telephones the Chief Constable, who confirms that there is no Inspector Goole in the police force. As far as Gerald and Mr and Mrs Birling are concerned, this changes everything, and all they have to do now is keep calm and avoid a public scandal.

Eric and Sheila are horrified at the attitude of the others: how they can ignore the fact that this girl is dead, and that they all helped to kill her?

BIRLING [*excitedly*]: By Jingo! A fake!

Birling

Birling and Gerald are determined to treat the incident as a hoax, or as some sort of practical joke. By doing this, they can reduce everything which has happened to the level of a stunt or trick.

Why should Birling be so pleased at Gerald's attitude? Remember that Birling is very conscious that Gerald and his family are, in Birling's eyes, socially superior to him.

ERIC: Whoever that chap was, the fact remains...

Eric has changed considerably during the course of the play, even during the course of this Act. Compare his responsibility and maturity now with the start of the Act, when he criticised Sheila for revealing the truth about his drunkenness: 'Why, you little sneak!'

Eric

BIRLING: Look – for God's sake!

Mr Birling finally loses patience with Sheila's determination to reveal their hypocrisy. It is a sad reflection on Mrs Birling's character that she is more upset by Birling's swearing than by anything she has been told during the evening.

GERALD: Did we? Who says so?

Think back across the events of the play and examine Gerald's reasoning here very carefully. Is he right that there is 'no more real evidence' that they all drove a girl to commit suicide than there is to prove that their visitor was a real police officer?

Was there more than one girl?

Gerald suggests that it may not even be just one girl – perhaps there were several. The Inspector never showed the photograph to more than one person at any one time. Gerald was not shown a photograph at all, and had simply admitted to knowing a girl called Daisy Renton. They have only the Inspector's word that this girl was Eva Smith. The girl did not use that name to Mrs Birling.

GERALD: We've no proof it was the same photograph...

Just how desperate the Birlings are to find a way of avoiding the truth is shown by their willingness to believe Gerald's theory.

If one regards the Inspector as a hoaxer (as Gerald and Mr Birling claim) Gerald's theory is highly unlikely. It is a preposterous set of wild coincidences to imagine that different girls got sacked by Birling, irritated Sheila, had affairs with Gerald and Eric and appeared before the charity organisation, all in the correct sequence, and then gave all the relevant information to the hoaxer. However, the Inspector does not strike the theatre audience as a hoaxer; nor do Eric and Sheila see him that way. If we regard him as some symbolic or spiritual figure, then Gerald's theory is perfectly likely, but irrelevant: the potential tragic consequences of their actions have been shown to all the characters.

GERALD: What girl? There were probably four or five...

The idea that up to five different girls might have been involved, one with each of the play's characters, seems incredible. But is it not equally unlikely that five people, all connected with the same family, should each have been involved with the same girl? Although Priestley has constructed his play as though it were realistic, it is in fact more like a fairy story or parable – a story with a hidden moral (a lesson) for us all.

ERIC: That doesn't matter to me...

Eric

Eric remains unmoved by the series of explanations which Gerald and Birling are busy developing. The girl whom he loved is dead; nothing else matters to him. At this point, Birling surprises the others by asking whether the girl really is dead: 'How do we know she is?' His question offers the characters another way out.

BIRLING: I'm convinced it is...

Notice Birling's reaction. He continues: 'No police inquiry. No one girl that all this happens to. No scandal –' It is left to Sheila to ask: 'And no suicide?'

Morality
If there is 'no one girl that all this happens to', does it make any difference to the guilt? In Priestley's morality, what are the Birlings guilty of?

Sheila

Birling

Notice that the girl's suicide is still uppermost in Sheila's mind.She will be overjoyed if it turns out that no pregnant young girl took her own life, because this is what has caused her most distress. But Birling is indifferent to the girl's death. If the fate of 'Eva' can be divided, so that several girls were involved, so much the better. The thought that, if this were true, it would mean that each of the girls suffered injustice, does not worry him. Nor does it occur to him that a pregnant young girl, about the same age as his daughter, died in the infirmary from an agonising suicide. All that concerns Birling is the avoidance of scandal.

GERALD: Anyway, we'll see. [*He goes to telephone...*]

Gerald

Gerald has appeared as a strong and confident character throughout. Notice, however, that even at the end he tries hard to wriggle out of his responsibility for the girl's fate. He tries to help Mr and Mrs Birling to do the same. Gerald still hopes to become engaged to Sheila, but sides with the Birlings at the end of the play. Why is this, do you think?

There is no suicide victim

Gerald and Mr Birling begin to wonder whether there really is a suicide case. Gerald telephones the Infirmary to check. They say they have no record of a girl who has died there that day: they have not had a suicide for months. Mr and Mrs Birling are delighted, as is Gerald. They are convinced that it has been an elaborate hoax. Mr Birling tells Sheila that it is all over now, but Sheila remains unconvinced. She cannot forget that all the things they confessed to really did happen. Mr Birling treats the Inspector's visit as a joke, and makes fun of the serious way Eric and Sheila took everything. Eric and Sheila are frightened by the way he talks. Sheila is upset that they had all seemed to be learning something, and now they have stopped.

BIRLING [*triumphantly*]: There you are! Proof positive...

Birling is triumphant: 'The whole story's just a lot of moonshine'. Before you decide that the whole story is too far-fetched to be true, consider how many real-life events might not be credible, if shown in the theatre.

BIRLING [*giving him a drink*]: Yes, he didn't...

Gerald has been out of the house for a while, to have a 'breather', and has had some time to think. Birling's use of words is revealing. What sort of person is usually described as 'on the run'?

SHEILA: No, because I remember what he said...

Sheila echoes the Inspector's threat of 'fire and blood and anguish'. In a traditional 'whodunnit' the criminal would be arrested: here, each 'criminal' must 'remember what he said', must change their ways, and must punish themselves by accepting the truth.

Gerald offers Sheila the ring again

Gerald thinks everything is back to normal, and offers the ring to Sheila. She refuses, saying that she must think about it.

GERALD: Everything's all right now, Sheila...

Gerald

Gerald assumes things can now return to where they were before the arrival of the Inspector. His offer of the ring echoes the same event from the start of the play. This time, significantly, Sheila refuses him. Another event from the start of the play is about to repeat itself.

Character

For the audience and two of the characters, the ending is unnecessary; the point has been made. As well as a dramatic final curtain, it makes sure that the unthinking, the unchanged, have a punishment to come.

The telephone rings – an Inspector is to call
Just as Mr Birling accuses Eric and Sheila of not being able to take a joke, the telephone rings. Birling answers it, then turns to the others, panic-stricken. It is the police. A girl has just died on her way to the Infirmary, having drunk some disinfectant. A police inspector is coming to call, to ask them some questions…

BIRLING: That was the police…

The final seconds of the play provide the final twist. It throws Gerald and Mr and Mrs Birling into confusion and makes a mockery of their elaborate self-congratulation. Are you glad that the culprits are about to get what they deserve, or do you sympathise with the Birlings' dilemma?

■ Self-test questions Act 3

Uncover the plot
Delete two of the three alternatives given, to find the correct plot. Beware possible misconceptions and muddles.

Eric tells how he bought Eva a meal/some drinks/some clothes but cannot speak about/forget/remember their love-making. His father is angry/distressed/ashamed and his mother is angry/shocked/hysterical when they hear of his theft. After the Inspector's departure, the family argue about responsibility/what to do/what has happened. Gradually, they begin to wonder about the Inspector's manner and Eric/Birling/Gerald confirms that he is not on the police force. Convinced that the whole affair was a hoax/joke/mistake, they begin to wonder if Eva was real/if Eva is dead/if they have imagined it. Gerald/Birling/Eric rings the Police Station/the police constable/the Infirmary; they haven't had a suicide for days/weeks/months. Gerald and Birling drink brandy/whisky/port to celebrate, while Sheila and Eric are still ashamed and feel angry/despairing/frightened at the way their elders are talking. A telephone call/a letter/the maid brings news that a girl has just died in the Infirmary/on her way to the Infirmary/in the operating theatre. The play ends in guilty/despairing/horrified silence.

Who? What? Why? When? When? Where? How?
1 Whom does Birling ring to question about the Inspector?
2 Who forgets most quickly the lesson about responsibility the Inspector has taught?
3 What is the Inspector's name?
4 What leads the Birlings to suspect that the Inspector is not all he seems?
5 Why does Gerald return?
6 Why did Eva let Eric into her apartment?
7 Where did Eric meet Eva?
8 How much money did Eric steal?
9 How did he get it?
10 How (according to Birling) will he repay it?

Who says?
1 'I never spoke to her'
2 'In a way she treated me – as if I were a kid.'

3   'And really, when I come to think of it, why you all had to go letting everything come out like that, beats me.'
4   'Well, he inspected us all right'
5   'You know, don't you?'

A question of responsibility

The word 'responsibility', with the concept it conveys, pervades the text. Can you find the following important quotations on this theme?

1   The Inspector's central statement in Act 3, just before he leaves.
2   Birling's speech just before the Inspector's first entrance in Act 1.
3   Birling's comment in Act 1 that describes responsibility as 'awkward'.
4   The Inspector's indication of the responsibilities of public figures in Act 2.
5   The Inspector's speech about shared responsibility in Act 2.

Parallel lines

Where do the following lines in Act 3 find echoes earlier in the play?

1   SHEILA: 'I suppose we're all nice people now.'
2   BIRLING: 'There'll be a public scandal… I was almost certain for a knighthood in the next honours list.'
3   GERALD: (*He holds up the ring*) 'What about this ring?'
4   BIRLING: 'That was the police. A girl has just died – on her way to the Infirmary – after swallowing some disinfectant, and a Police Inspector is on his way here – to ask some – questions –.'

Questions on the whole play

1   Who (in your opinion) is the most sensitive member of the Birling family?
2   Immediately after the Inspector's exit, most of the family try to regain the certainties they had at the beginning of the play. Which aspects of their relationships are permanently altered?
3   The action of the play is continuous and the general outline of the 'chain of events' becomes apparent fairly early in the play. How does Priestley use suspense to create dramatic tension?
4   What is the Inspector's relationship to reality?
5   What is the effect of the end of the play?

■ How to write a coursework essay

Most of you are probably studying *An Inspector Calls* as part of your GCSE English Literature coursework for the assignment on twentieth-entury drama. In writing your essay there are certain requirements which must be met. In particular, you must show awareness (though not necessarily at great length) of social, historical and cultural contexts and of literary conventions.

You will find that the social/historical/cultural element in essays on *An Inspector Calls* is easy to include: there will be references to class, moral and political views or historical events in almost any essay on the play. The strongest literary conventions you could consider here are the 'whodunnit' and the naturalistic drama. You should show awareness of how Priestley twists both traditions: a 'whodunnit' with five guilty parties and no actual crime, and a naturalistic play turned on its head by a figure from another world (another age?). In addition, the section of this book on **Structure** relates *An Inspector Calls* to the Greek tradition of drama.

It is also essential that you show considerable evidence of textual knowledge, even if the essay has a strong creative element. Types of response might include:

- analysis of character;
- relating the text to its social or historical context;
- study of one or more productions;
- empathic response to character;
- creation of an additional scene.

If you are writing an analytical essay, the most important consideration is that you must develop an argument or explain a point of view throughout. There is nothing to be gained by repeating what the Inspector says. What is important is that you relate it to your theme: Priestley's political views, or the reaction of the Birlings, or the dramatic effect of a certain scene, etc. You should make a decision on what each paragraph is about, as far as possible signalling this to the reader in the opening sentence, often called a *topic sentence* because it introduces the topic of the paragraph.

If you choose an imaginative/creative essay, the first essential is to reveal throughout your factual knowledge of the text and a soundly based interpretation of it. Mere imagination will not gain credit in textual study for GCSE English Literature.

The length of your essay will depend on the type of essay you write, your own wishes and your teacher's advice, but do bear in mind that it is only one of several pieces of coursework: there is no need for a 5000 word blockbuster.

Character analysis

The characters of the Birlings (plus Gerald Croft) are obviously central to the play, and a coursework essay could well consider them in one form or another. The use of contrast is so effective that it is wiser to deal with all five rather than to single one or two out. The question of **Guilt** would be an appropriate subject, and is considered in **How to write an examination essay** (which contains ideas that could also be appropriate to your coursework). Let us examine a straightforward character assignment:

> *Examine the characters of the Birlings and Gerald Croft, considering how far they share the characteristics of their class and how they respond to the Inspector's revelations.*

As the question is set, there are three distinct elements. The first is not at all difficult: you have to point out what sort of people the five are. J B Priestley is more than helpful: even before the first line is spoken, he has given a clue to each of them in the opening stage directions. Mrs Birling, for instance, is 'rather cold and her husband's social superior' (a very helpful start), Eric is 'not quite at ease, half shy, half assertive', and so on. But, in proving all your points, don't forget that it is essential to bring in evidence, in the form of quotation or reference.

More challenging is the question about the characteristics of their class. (Incidentally you should note that Gerald and Mrs Birling are of a rather higher class.) As Priestley presents it, these seem to be vanity, self-satisfaction, neglect of others, refusal to take responsibility for their actions and other undesirable qualities. (You may find the shape of the essay is helped by considering these first and then moving on to individuals.) How far do all the characters share these? Sheila emerges as a sympathetic character, but how can you describe her behaviour in Milward's? Is there any sign of her conscience before the Inspector appears? What about poor guilt-ridden Eric? Was he going to confess that he was a thief? Has he ever considered the consequences of his actions? Or are all five (before the Inspector's arrival) as bad as each other?

It is important that you explain rather than just narrate. You should consider the response to the Inspector on a generational basis. The young are less hardened, more impressionable, and you will be able to explain the various responses in this light. Gerald, a little older, belongs much more in the senior Birlings' camp in his response (though it is worth remembering that his original guilt is less than Eric's or Sheila's).

It is, of course, perfectly possible to write an essay on **Inspector Goole**. If you choose to do this, you will need to avoid a conventional character study and consider his *role* in the play: in other words, what he achieves, what his methods are and, above all, some speculation (but no assertions) on who or what he is.

Character empathy

Over the years an extremely popular essay in GCSE coursework has been to write *Eva Smith's Diary*. This is perfectly acceptable, but should be approached with caution. It has sometimes inspired extended entries day-by-day from the first inkling of the strike to the aftermath of the refusal at the Charity Organisation, often heavily factual, revealing little interpretation. Laborious to write and to read, this offers little insight. If you choose this subject, it would help to be selective about entries, but above all you must show understanding of the play. There are enough indications of the character of Eva for the diarist to be convincing; her impressions of the other characters must reflect what Priestley shows of them; above all, the background and social attitudes must be authentic. This is not easy, but an Eva Smith who acts and talks like a Nineties teenager gains little credit.

Why not look for some other way of extending a character (or characters) outside Priestley's scenes? You might choose Sheila at Milward's (dramatic scene, or maybe diary), the build-up to the parting of Gerald and Daisy (letters, perhaps) or the meeting of the Charity Organisation (dramatic scene), to mention only a few. Remember it is *essential* that the character is recognisable from the play and that events in the play are not changed: if you invent anything, it *must* be possible within Priestley's framework.

Morality

An Inspector Calls *has been described at different times as a sermon and 'a lesson in civics'. How far can the play be viewed simply as a vehicle for Priestley's moral and political views?*

You should be able, without too much difficulty, to find examples of Priestley's moral and political views in the play, but there are two essential elements which you need to consider if you choose this, or a similar, topic.

Firstly, it is important to explain clearly what these views of Priestley were and, if possible, find examples of his writing elsewhere which develop them. For example, in *Thoughts in the Wilderness* (1957), he wrote, 'A man is a member of a community and the fact that he is a member of a community immensely enlarges his stature and increases his opportunities.' In his war-time talks (published as *Postscripts*) he stressed again and again the importance of liberty, democracy and faith in ordinary people. He believed in responsibility (for ourselves and for others) and preached a caring type of Socialism.

Secondly, you will need to show that this presentation of moral issues strengthens, not weakens, the drama. It has been suggested that *An Inspector Calls* is like a medieval morality play where we enjoy the overthrow of sin. Certainly we enjoy the overthrow of several, possibly all Seven, Deadly Sins (most satisfyingly, Pride) in *An Inspector Calls*. Also, the play is a mystery thriller where we are not looking at actual crimes, but at moral failings. What, therefore, creates the very real tension in the later stages of the play?

Productions

Comparison of productions is another possible essay topic. It is desirable that your GCSE studies should show awareness of the text as drama, not just the printed page. If you are able to see the production referred to in the section, *An Inspector Calls*: **1912–1945** and compare it to, say, a television version, you will find plenty of material.

It is important to remember that writing about productions commits you to thinking about the interpretation, why things are done a certain way, and what that suggests about the play. Comments on the fact that a certain actor is good (or bad) will only take you part of the way.

How to write an examination essay

Some of you may be required to answer an examination question on *An Inspector Calls*. This section considers one specific title on the play, but also gives general advice on how to approach an English Literature essay. Remember that the question considered could also be used as a coursework essay, and indeed the titles in the **Coursework** section on **Character analysis** and **Morality** could be set in an examination.

> *Who, in your opinion, is most responsible for the death of Eva Smith? Compare and contrast the characters and actions of the five central characters (the Birling family and Gerald Croft), using evidence from the text to justify your opinion.*

Before you start writing

- The first essential is thorough revision. It is important that you realise that even Open Book examinations require close textual knowledge. You will have time to look up quotations and references, but *only if you know where to look.*

- Read the questions very carefully, both to choose the best one and to take note of exactly what you are asked to do.

- Do not answer the question you imagine or hope has been set. In the case of the title we are considering, note that it asks who is *most responsible*, not who is the *worst person*. Motives and character do matter, but it is not a simple judgement. The most sympathetic character among the Birlings is Sheila, the least sympathetic is Mrs Birling, but which one plunged Eva from happiness to despair and which one took her the shorter journey from despair to deeper despair? Also, note the demand for textual evidence.

- Identify all the key words in the question that mention characters, events and themes, and instructions as to what to do: e.g. compare, contrast, comment, give an account, etc. Write a short list of the things you have to do. Here key words include *compare* and *contrast*, but not 'give an account': story-telling is not required. Another key phrase is *justify your opinion*. There is no right answer: it remains an opinion, but it must be justifiable.

- Look at the points you have identified and jot down what you are going to say about each. On what grounds, for instance, are you going to compare the actions of the characters: their motives, perhaps, the effect on Eva, how final this effect was, etc.

- Decide in what order you are going to deal with the main points. Number them in sequence. This is a matter of choice, but do not use chronological order ('First Eva gets sacked by Mr Birling ...') unless you have a good reason to.

Writing the essay

- The first sentences are important. Try to summarise your response to the question so the examiner has some idea of how you plan to approach it. For example, 'The responsibility for Eva Smith's death is shared almost equally among the members of the family group, but it is possible to separate the guilt of malice and pride from the thoughtlessness of weakness and selfishness.' Jump straight into the essay; do not nibble at the edges for a page and a half. A personal response is rewarded (especially in essays like this, where there is *no right answer*), but you must always answer the question – as you write your essay, refer back to your list of points.

- Answer *all* of the question. Many students spend all their time answering just one part of a question and ignoring the rest. This prevents you gaining marks for the parts left out. In the same way, failing to answer enough questions on the examination is a waste of marks which can always be gained most easily at the start of an answer.

- There is no 'correct' length for an essay. What you must do is to spend the full time usefully in answering all parts of the question: spending longer than the allocated time by more than a few minutes is dangerous. It is an advantage if you can organise your time so well as to reach an elegant conclusion: in this case, perhaps moving the essay on from an examination of responsibility to Priestley's emphasis on the need to learn from guilt. However, it is better to leave an essay without a conclusion than to fail to get started on the next question.

- Use quotation or paraphrase when it is relevant and contributes to the quality and clarity of your answer. In this case, there is no need for precise quotation about events. Sentences or phrases that express the characters' attitudes and motives, an acceptance or rejection of guilt or a precise response to Eva are much more useful: 'I was quite justified.' (Birling) 'So I'm really responsible?' (Sheila) 'I blame the young man who was the father of the child ...' (Mrs Birling) etc. Nearly always extended quotations are unhelpful and are often used as padding, which is a complete waste of time.

Uncover the plot

The Birling family are having a dinner to celebrate Sheila's engagement to Gerald. They pass round the port and Gerald gives Sheila a ring. Edna announces the Inspector, who brings news of the suicide of a young woman two hours previously in the Infirmary. She was called Eva Smith and her death was agonising. Mr Birling recognises her photograph; he sacked her nearly two years ago because she asked for a wage increase of 2s and 6d. She got a job in a clothes shop, but was dismissed after two months because of a complaint from a customer. It was Sheila – recognising the photograph, she leaves the room in tears. The Inspector refuses to show Gerald the photograph but Sheila observes that he knows Eva's assumed name, Daisy Renton, and forces him to admit that Eva was his mistress. She laughs hysterically when he asks her not to reveal this and tells him the Inspector already knows the truth.

Who? What? Why? When? When? Where? How?

1 Eric and Sheila (Gerald supports Birling)
2 Birling
3 Lord Mayor (two years ago)
4 They are 'friendly rivals in business'
5 Because – like an ordinary Inspector – he is 'on duty'
6 Both her parents were dead and she had no money
7 End of September, 1910 (nearly two years before the action of the play)
8 At Milwards, a fashionable clothes shop
9 She commits suicide by drinking disinfectant
10 She is distressed, asks if it was an accident and then says: 'Oh I wish you hadn't told me'

Who is this?

1 Inspector Goole
2 Arthur Birling
3 Eric Birling
4 Sheila Birling
5 Gerald Croft
6 Sybil Birling

Who says?

1 Edna, the maid
2 Birling
3 Gerald
4 Sheila

Hidden agendas

1 Near the beginning, Sheila says 'so you be careful' to Gerald and Eric 'suddenly guffaws'. He is unable to explain this.
2 When the Inspector is announced, Gerald jokes that maybe Eric has been up to something. Eric's reaction is sharp and uneasy.
3 When Gerald and Birling are discussing womens' clothes and how they affect their self-esteem, Eric breaks in eagerly: 'Yes, I remember –', then checks himself. Again, he is unable to explain.
4 Eric is uneasy with the Inspector, bursting out that he's had enough of the enquiry. He wants to go to bed, but the Inspector insists that he remain.

5 Note the clues throughout the Act that Eric is drinking quite heavily (for example, he helps himself to another glass of port while talking to Gerald and his father). This is another sign that he is worried and feeling guilty. Sheila reveals in Act 2 that he has a drink problem.

Open quotes
1 'That's what I asked myself when I was looking at that dead girl. And then I said to myself, "Well, we'll try to understand why it had to happen".'
2 'I did nothing. She's upsetting herself.'
3 'Yes, but you can't. It's too late. She's dead.'
4 'That's more or less what I was thinking earlier tonight, when I was in the infirmary looking at what was left of Eva Smith. A nice little promising life there, I thought, and a nasty mess somebody's made of it.'
5 'Sometimes there isn't as much difference as you think. Often, if it was left to me, I wouldn't know where to draw the line.'

■ Self-test answers Act 2

Uncover the plot
The Inspector dismisses Sheila but she refuses to go; she and Gerald bicker. The secret of Eric's drinking is revealed and Mrs Birling is staggered. Gerald tells how he met Eva in the Palace music hall; she wanted to talk and he found some food for her. He says that he felt sorry for her; the affair ended in September. Gerald leaves to take a walk, saying he will return. Mrs Birling pretends not to recognise the photograph, although Sheila realises she is lying. They are interrupted by news of Eric's departure – the Inspector is angry and Mr and Mrs Birling frightened. The questioning continues; Eva was pregnant when Mrs Birling was responsible for help being refused her. Mrs Birling describes her story as 'ridiculous' and thinks that the father of the child should be dealt with 'severely'. It is Sheila who first realises Eric is the father; as the curtain falls, he enters, looking 'pale and distressed' and his mother gives a little cry.

Who? What? Why? When? When? Where? How?
1 Alderman Meggarty
2 The father of her unborn child
3 She had no money and, because pregnant, could find no work
4 She returns the engagement ring he gave her earlier
5 She does not wish to be implicated in the girl's suicide
6 Two weeks before the action of the play at a committee meeting for a Women's Charity Organisation
7 To a place by the sea
8 He has her diary

Who says to whom?
1 The Inspector, to Mrs Birling
2 Mrs Birling (about Eva), answering Sheila
3 Sheila, to Gerald
4 Sheila, to her mother
5 Gerald, to the Inspector

Mutual recrimination
1 Sheila, to her mother (Act 2)
2 Eric, to Sheila (Act 1)
3 Sheila, to her father (Act 1)
4 Mrs Birling, about Gerald's affair with Eva (Act 2)
5 Birling, to Eric (Act 3)

Saying no
1 MRS BIRLING (*of Eric*): 'He's only a boy'. INSPECTOR: 'No, he's a young man'
2 MRS BIRLING: 'I don't understand you, Inspector.' INSPECTOR: 'You mean you don't choose to, Mrs Birling.' MRS BIRLING (*angrily*): 'I meant what I said.' INSPECTOR: 'You're not telling me the truth.'
3 MRS BIRLING (*to Sheila*): 'I don't understand you. (To the Inspector) Do you?' INSPECTOR: 'Yes. And she's right.'
4 BIRLING (*about Eric's departure*): 'he was in one of his excitable queer moods, and even though we don't need him here–' INSPECTOR (cutting in sharply): 'We do need him here.'
5 MRS BIRLING: 'if I prefer not to discuss it any further, you have no power to make me change my mind.' INSPECTOR: 'Yes, I have.'

Open quotes
1 SHEILA (*with irony*): 'That was nice for you.' GERALD: 'No it wasn't.'
2 INSPECTOR: 'You have no hope of not discussing it, Mrs Birling.'
3 SHEILA: 'Just what I was going to ask.' BIRLING: (*rising, angrily*): 'I really must protest –' INSPECTOR: (*turning on him sharply*): 'Why should you do any protesting?'
4 INSPECTOR 'Not yet. I'm waiting.' MRS BIRLING: 'Waiting for what?' INSPECTOR: 'To do my duty.'
5 GERALD: 'If possible – yes.' INSPECTOR: 'Well, we know one young woman who wasn't, don't we?'

■ Self-test answers Act 3

Uncover the plot
Eric tells how he bought Eva some drinks but cannot remember their love-making. His father is angry and his mother is shocked when they hear of his theft. After the Inspector's departure, the family argue about responsibility. Gradually, they begin to wonder about the Inspector's manner and Gerald confirms that he is not on the police force. Convinced that the whole affair was a hoax, they begin to wonder if Eva is dead. Gerald rings the Infirmary; they haven't had a suicide for months. Gerald and Birling drink whisky to celebrate, while Sheila and Eric are still ashamed and feel frightened at the way their elders are talking. A telephone call brings news that a girl has just died on her way to the Infirmary. The play ends in guilty silence.

Who? What? Why? When? When? Where? How?
1 The Chief Constable, Colonel Roberts
2 Mr and Mrs Birling
3 Goole
4 They realise that he arrived after Birling's speech about everyone minding his or her own business; they recall his manner: police inspectors 'don't talk like that.'

5 He met a police sergeant on his walk, who swore there was no Inspector Goole in the local force.
6 Because he was drunk and threatened to make a row.
7 In the Palace bar, where Gerald has been with her on an earlier occasion.
8 About fifty pounds.
9 From the office; collecting small accounts, he gave the firm's receipt and kept the cash.
10 He will work for nothing until every penny is repaid.

Who says?
1 The Inspector (about Eva)
2 Eric (about Eva)
3 Birling (to all his family)
4 Sheila (as to whether the Inspector was 'real')
5 Eric (to all those present)

A question of responsibility
1 'We are responsible for each other. And I tell you that the time will soon come when, if men will not learn that lesson, then they will be taught it in fire and blood and anguish' (Act 3).
2 'the way some of these cranks talk and write now, you'd think everybody has to look after everybody else, as if we were all mixed up together like bees in a hive-community…' (Act1).
3 'If we were all responsible for everything that happened to everybody we'd had anything to do with, it would be very awkward, wouldn't it?' (Act 1).
4 'Public men, Mr Birling, have responsibilities as well as privileges' (Act 2).
5 'Now Miss Birling has just been made to understand what she did to this girl. She feels responsible. And if she leaves us now, and doesn't hear any more, she'll be alone with her responsibility, the rest of tonight, all tomorrow, all the next night – …You see, we have to share something. If there's nothing else, we'll have to share our guilt.' (Act 2).

Parallel lines
1 GERALD: 'You seem to be a nice well-behaved family' (Act 1).
2 BIRLING: '…So – well – I gather there's a very good chance of a knighthood – so long as we behave ourselves, don't get into the police court or start a scandal – eh?' (Act 1).
3 Gerald gives Sheila the ring early in Act 1 and she returns it in Act 2.
4 This takes the play full circle back to Edna: 'Please sir, an inspector's called' (Act 1).

Questions on the whole play
1 It is usually Sheila, who first senses the hypocrisy and lies of the others.
2 Eric's drinking is now in the open and his mother will no longer be able to describe him as 'just a boy.' He and Sheila have formed a new bond of honesty against their parents. Will Sheila and Gerald patch up their engagement? If they do, it will be upon a completely new footing – they 'aren't the same people.'
3 Priestley uses interruptions, exits and entrances to build suspense, balancing people who know the truth with people who don't. At the beginning, the audience is in complete ignorance; piece by piece, the Inspector builds up his chain of evidence. Each Act ends with a moment of dramatic tension.
4 The play appears to be realistic, but we are not surprised when the Inspector turns out not to be a 'real' Police Inspector – his role is larger than, not less than, reality: he is a moral force. Sheila: 'I don't know much about police

inspectors – but the ones I have met weren't a bit like you… perhaps they ought to have been. As if – suddenly – there came a real one – at last' (Act 2).

There is a sense in which this is a morality play, with characters who are types.

5 Priestley's surprise, time-lapse ending gives a grim ending to the play. The play's continuous action and the massive figure of the Inspector give An Inspector Calls a strong feeling of inevitability. Although many characters leave the stage, they all feel impelled to return. Even Gerald does not escape. The ending intensifies this claustrophobic, trapped feeling.

Notes

Notes

Notes

Notes

Notes